"Have dinner with me tonight?"

Lyon's voice, warm and coaxing, sent shivers up Colleen's spine. She swayed against him unsteadily, wanting to say no but unable to.

As if sensing her doubts, Lyon pulled her closer still, until their bodies touched in one long electric line. "We could go somewhere quiet, somewhere out of the way," he continued in a seductive whisper.

Succumbing to the dizzying sensations engulfing her, Colleen wrapped her arms around his neck. The last of her inhibitions dissolved as Lyon's mouth met hers, and she arched sensuously against him, the heat of her kiss matching his.

Just as she thought she would drown in the depth of her desire, Lyon drew back slightly. On a ragged breath he murmured, "Does that mean you're hungry?"

THE AUTHOR

Cathy Gillen Thacker began her writing
career with one short story. Now, some ten
years and eight published books later, she
has established herself as a successful
romance author.

"I believe that love is the one thing people
should never have to do without," says
Cathy. Happily married with three children,
she has a lot of love in her own life.

Books by Cathy Gillen Thacker

These books may be available at your local bookseller.

Don't miss any of our special offers. Write to us at the
following address for information on our newest releases.

Harlequin Reader Service
P.O. Box 52040, Phoenix, AZ 85072-2040
Canadian address: P.O. Box 2800, Postal Station A,
5170 Yonge St., Willowdale, Ont. M2N 6J3

A Private Passion

CATHY GILLEN THACKER

Harlequin Books

TORONTO • NEW YORK • LONDON
AMSTERDAM • PARIS • SYDNEY • HAMBURG
STOCKHOLM • ATHENS • TOKYO • MILAN

To Jerry, Elvira and Joanna Aynesworth
and all my friends at
the Anderson Mill Book Exchange.

Published November 1985

ISBN 0-373-25182-3

1

COLLEEN CHANDLER knew the moment she saw him that she should never have agreed to cut Lyon Haggerty's hair, no matter how high the fee promised her. Butterflies danced riotously in her midriff and she tingled from head to toe after just one look at the man.

"Hi," he drawled softly, opening the door a shade farther and leaning one broad shoulder against the frame. Still slightly breathless from her dash through the crowded downtown streets of Columbus, Colleen was perspiring faintly after the switch from brisk outdoor air to the centrally heated interior of the exclusive Regency Hotel. At the sound of his marvelously deep voice, the heels of her suede boots dug an inch deeper into the thick oyster-gray carpet of the wide hallway between the penthouse and the elevator. She wished she had something to hang on to; her knees felt treacherously weak and unsteady, as if she was standing on the deck of a pitching ship.

"Hi." Further speech eluded her. Not usually one to be thrown off balance by one glance at any man, she was nonetheless captivated by Lyon Haggerty's palpable self-assurance and surprisingly pleasant, warm demeanor. She'd expected someone artsy-craftsy, even weird. He was neither.

His gaze drifted over the Nordic paleness of her chin-length hair and lingered on the feathery bangs that framed her oval face, before returning approvingly to her thick-lashed eyes. "You must be Colleen. Sorry about the last-minute call for an out-of-salon appointment, but I wasn't sure when I would be free."

Clutching the strap of the tote bag full of equipment she had slung over her shoulder, Colleen gave him what she hoped was a coolly professional, purposeful nod. "That's perfectly all right, Mr. Haggerty." Hers was a service industry and she prided herself on giving clients the excellent care to which her high fees entitled them.

Lyon Haggerty's sensual chiseled lips parted in a smile, revealing beautiful, even white teeth. "Call me Lyon," he said in that remarkable voice.

For the second time since she'd set eyes on him, Colleen's breath left her lungs in a rush. "Lyon." She smiled, relaxing only slightly, despite his efforts to put her at ease. Stepping back, he ushered her wordlessly into the VIP suite, shut the door behind them, then led the way into the center of the sumptuously appointed room. She followed obediently, almost trotting to keep up with his long lazy strides.

He was a tall man, easily six foot one or two—a good seven inches taller than she—with a lithe muscular frame and easy grace. Up close, he looked just as self-possessed and intense as all his publicity photos portrayed him. He was wearing dark-blue French jeans that molded his hips and thighs like a second, very flattering skin. His white silk shirt, worn open at the throat, was obviously custom made. A narrow blue tie was knotted loosely below his collarbone. His shirtsleeves were rolled to just below the elbows, revealing a light covering of tawny hair over strong forearms. The hair on his head—the most glorious shade of wheat-gold Colleen had ever seen—was thick, wavy and totally unruly. He hadn't been exaggerating when he'd said he needed a haircut.

In an effort to compose herself, she unbuttoned her blue-gray suede jacket and smoothed the fluffy layers of her wind-tossed hair into place with a single accomplished sweep of her palm.

"You don't mind working in my hotel room?" For a moment he seemed just as uncomfortable as she. They were, after all, total strangers yet here they stood, alone in his hotel room, preparing to undertake a rather intimate chore. There weren't even any other guests permitted on this floor.

"Not at all," she assured him. Colleen had become accustomed to the whims of celebrities while living and working on the east coast several years before. Lyon's request that she come here simply stemmed from a desire for privacy, she knew. In an attempt to fight down her reaction to the blatant masculinity emanating from him, she surveyed her surroundings.

Decorated in shades of white, gold and blue, the suite was as sleekly elegant and modern as the building itself. Geometric prints decorated the slate-blue walls of the sitting room. Through the open door of the adjacent bedroom, though, she could see clothing, suitcases and stacks of paper strewn about. Charcoal storyboards were set up on an easel next to the bed. She smiled, realizing the man had at least one flaw—he was messy.

"You've done this often, then?" His eyebrows rose with the question.

"Yes. I dealt with a number of celebrities during the years I lived in New York, and lately I've been seeing quite a few out-of-salon clients in Columbus."

"Anyone I might know?" he inquired.

Who didn't Lyon know? A list of his luncheon companions alone would probably read like a "Who's Who" of both Hollywood and New York acting communities. Colleen didn't monitor the movie industry the way her younger sister, Amy, did, but even she knew that in less than five years Lyon had turned the film industry upside down, producing one runaway hit after another. To the astonishment and envy of his colleagues, he'd made millions for himself, his stars and the two rival film companies for which he worked.

Forcing herself to display a nonchalance she was far from feeling, Colleen answered in a deceptively velvet voice. "The lead singer of the rock group, Cancelled Check, visiting newsmen. Occasionally I work for soap-opera stars who are in town to do dinner theatre."

"The manager at the front desk said you were the best stylist in the city. Where did you get your training?" His gaze was pleasant but alert. She had the feeling he didn't miss a single detail.

"I was licensed here at City College. After that I worked for Monsieur Marc in New York."

"And quit to come back to Columbus, Ohio?" He seemed mystified by her choice of location to settle down.

"I wanted to open my own salon, and though I had some capital I didn't have enough to establish a first-rate shop in New York," she explained. At first she had missed the dazzling penthouses, the haute couture, the close contact with celebrities and politicians. But in the final analysis, a client's fame or lack of it made no difference in terms of the satisfaction she derived from her job. To Colleen, each person represented a unique challenge; each successful styling or hair design was a source of personal pride.

He smiled. "How do you like being your own boss?"

"I love it." His cologne was tantalizingly fresh and brisk, like the combination of fir trees and new-fallen snow on a cold winter's day. She let the strap of her bag slide from her shoulder, down her arm, and caught it in the palm of her hand. Temporarily free of the weight she'd been carrying, she relaxed.

Meanwhile Lyon was perusing her with infinite interest. His long-lashed gaze swept over her pleated navy trousers and stylish boots, powder-blue silk shirt visible beneath her jacket, and finally returned to her face. "You're not upset to be working so late on a Friday evening?"

"No. I had nothing else planned." Belatedly she realized she'd told him too much.

His voice held a note of speculation and surprise. "No date?"

"No. Shall we get started?"

Lyon directed her perfunctorily toward the plush bathroom. As they moved through the doorway the tips of his fingers lightly brushed her shoulder in a guiding motion. "I thought we'd set up in here if it's all right with you." A seven-foot marble tub took up one wall, a glassed-in shower stall another and a vanity ran the twelve-foot length of the room. The commode was separated by another door, which Lyon shut. Suddenly the room seemed smaller, his presence more arresting, compelling. A shiver of awareness slid down her spine. "This is fine." Colleen set her tote down on the counter next to the sink.

One hand working free the buttons of his shirt, Lyon removed his tie with the other and sighed as if he was not looking forward to the haircut. Vaguely amused by his reluctance, a feeling shared by many first-time customers, Colleen shrugged out of her jacket. Aware of his eyes upon her, she folded the garment neatly, put it on the far edge of the counter and turned to face him.

He was leaning with one shoulder against the wall, his hand on a button at midchest. He paused, his glance touching on her ringless left hand, then moving to her face. He appeared pleased to see she wore no wedding or engagement ring. "What do you do in your spare time?"

"Read, practice gourmet cooking. Take care of my seventeen-year-old sister, Amy." His eyes held hers in silent inquiry, and she explained, "My parents died three years ago. Their car went off a road during a snowstorm when they were on holiday. I've been guardian to Amy ever since." A responsibility that, more than anything else, had dictated the specifics of her life.

"Another reason you returned to the Midwest?" he asked, gently, his gaze not wavering from hers. Lyon's eyes were the most arresting shade of amber, not all brown as she'd thought at first glance, but flecked with tiny lights of gold that seemed to match the rich wheat shade of his hair.

"Yes." She accepted his tacit sympathy graciously, then steered the conversation away from herself. "Have you been enjoying your stay in Columbus?"

"I haven't been here but a few hours." Eyes shuttering slightly, he folded his arms across his chest in a relaxed pose.

She was struck again by the incredible awareness in his face, the compassion and watchful intelligence also reflected in his work. Feeling as spineless as a marshmallow, she struggled to remember the precise names of his films. She and Amy had watched many of them on cable television, but to her irritation her mind was a blank, her memory as elusive and unreliable as her ability to converse normally. "I've seen all of your movies," she ventured.

"Which was your favorite?" His mouth curved into a delicious smile. She noticed the full lower lip and the strong line of his jaw, slightly shadowed by an evening beard.

"It's difficult to decide." She unzipped her tote with more care than usual and took out a plastic cape, sterile combs, scissors, a brush and a packet of salon shampoo. "Actually," she continued, recalling the story lines of his diverse collection of movies. "I liked them all very much."

Shoving himself away from the wall, he grinned. "Even the one about the aliens from outer space?"

He moved so he was standing behind her, and Colleen watched him in the mirror. She noticed the way the fabric of his shirt gently molded his body, wished he had never taken off his tie, even more strongly wished away the insane desire to reach out and part the edges of his partially unbuttoned shirt and touch the solid-looking masculine chest beneath the cloth. Still watching her, he moved around to sit on the edge of the marble counter, facing her, leaning back on his hands.

Belatedly remembering his question, she replied quickly, "Yes. I liked *Space Raiders* very much." An unexpected wave of pleasure washed through her, weakening her knees. Warmth stole into her cheeks.

"What about *Restless Spirits*?" With the toe of his boot he nudged a tile line on the floor. He seemed to be leashing his energy with effort.

"I thought you did a great job of depicting suburban life, both before and after it had gone awry." With effort, she reminded herself she had been hired to do a job, not to converse with the client. "Now, what can I do for you?" she asked, brandishing her comb. To her relief, her voice sounded composed. "My receptionist said you wanted a trim."

"Right." He fingered the silken layers of hair that brushed his collar and his brows, and almost covered his ears, then looked at her expectantly. "I want it out of my eyes and off my neck. To be honest, I don't want to have to get another haircut for a couple of months if I can help it."

She grinned. At least he was straightforward about his neglect of his tresses. Though, to his credit, his hair didn't look the least bit damaged. It was just overly long.

He pulled the hem of his shirt from his pants, undid the last buttons and slid it off his shoulders to reveal a firm muscled torso covered sparsely with golden-brown hair. Despite her determination to show no reaction, Colleen felt her breath catch in her throat. No doubt about it, she sighed inwardly, the man was as magnificently formed and maintained as any of the sought-after movie idols he directed. It suddenly seemed incredible that he was real and breathing and only inches away. Trying to recover from her immediate physical response to his partial nudity but all too aware of her damp palms and the tingling sensations in her middle, she fumbled through her tote for an extra pair of shears—ones she knew she wouldn't need—and an extra container of shampoo.

With an overhand loop, Lyon tossed his shirt onto the clear-glass shower door. Grimacing, he explained his actions. "Getting hair under my shirt makes me itch like crazy."

She nodded sympathetically, still feeling unaccountably nervous, then moved closer to wind a length of tissue paper around his neck. "This will keep most of the stray hairs off your skin."

He stood absolutely still, muscles tense as she worked. His gaze wandered down to linger on the swell of her breasts beneath the clinging fabric of her shirt, moved toward her waist, then abruptly shifted to the outer room. Except for the faint movement of his throat as he swallowed, he seemed hardly to be aware of her presence as she draped a terry-cloth towel around his shoulders. She wished she could say the same for herself. At his proximity her nipples had tightened, peaking against the thin silk of her blouse, barely restrained by her scanty lace bra.

She ordered herself to concentrate on the task at hand. So he was handsome, so he was virile, so he was...starkly sexual. So what? Teeth grinding, she forced a smile, then drew a deep breath, trying to ignore the fact that since he'd faced her he hadn't taken his eyes off her. "Okay, next question. How do you want to do this?"

With a casual wave of his hand he left the decision-making process to her. She surveyed the room. Her hand resting lightly on her hip, she glanced from the large twin sinks stretched along the marble countertop to the oversize tub. Neither provided a comfortable working space for a shampoo, and though she was used to such strategical problems whenever she accepted an out-of-salon assignment, they somehow seemed amplified now.

Aloud, she mused quietly, still feeling awkward and ill-at-ease, "I'd like to wash your hair first."

Lyon pivoted toward the sink; it was too small to allow him to rinse his hair directly beneath the faucet. He turned toward the tub that, although large enough, would require him to kneel on the floor with Colleen over him. "I hadn't given much thought to this," he admitted, his mouth twisting wryly. "Maybe the easiest thing would be for me to just jump in the shower." He reached nonchalantly for the brief blue kimono that was hanging from a hook on the door.

Colleen didn't want to be that informal. Just the thought of him naked and damp beneath the thin blue silk made her thighs turn to jelly. She swallowed hard. "I think I can wash your hair in the sink if you'll just pull up a chair and bend forward." Miraculously, her voice sounded calm and controlled.

He went into the other room to get the chair. She successfully fought both a blush and a sigh of relief. Her expression was deceptively noncommittal when he returned and seated himself in front of the sink, his feet straddling either side of the chair.

She adjusted the water temperature to warm, all the while staring down at his broad back. She couldn't help wondering if his chest felt as solid and muscular as it looked beneath the draping of fluffy white terry. And if so, how it would feel to be held by him, her breasts crushed against that hard surface? She wondered whether he would be an aggressive or a gentle lover, if he would bring the same skill and sensitivity to his lovemaking as he did to his films. She couldn't imagine any woman being able to summon up the strength to resist this man, knowing even now how deliciously and unexpectedly wanton he made her feel.

She immediately banished that last thought. She would never make love with a man casually. To do so was to invite hurt.

Using a small water pitcher next to the sink, Colleen painstakingly began to wet Lyon's hair. He was silent, his eyes closed as she poured shampoo onto the center of her palm and with sweeping circular motions worked it into the thick layers of his hair.

His low sigh echoed through both his rangy body and the room, dangerously stirring her senses again. Growling his pleasure at the skillful massaging of her hands, he murmured, "Mmm, that feels good."

To her surprise—she had done this hundreds, no thousands, of times before—there was something incredibly sensual and intimate about working her fingers through his hair. And as she worked she felt the muscles in his neck and back relax.

Methodically she rinsed and then shampooed a second time, delighting in the luxuriantly thick silky hair beneath her palms. She finished with a soothing warm-water rinse and then reached for another thick, fluffy bath towel and gently patted his hair damp-dry. She nudged his shoulders lightly to signal she was through and he sat up, blinking as if he'd been asleep.

He faced the vanity mirror. Certain she could hear the furious pounding of her heart, she pulled a comb through his tangled hair. Finished, she ran through the routine questions necessary before she could begin cutting. "Do you usually blow your hair dry or just let it dry naturally?"

"I blow it dry if I have the time. If I'm rushed I just rub it with a towel, comb it into place and let it go." He passed his knuckles over his jaw in a restless gesture and leaned farther back into his chair. The fabric of his jeans stretched tightly across the bunched muscles in his thighs, emphasizing the flat expanse of his abdomen beneath the thin hand-crafted leather belt.

Colleen dragged her eyes back to his unsmiling countenance in the mirror. "When you blow it dry, do you use a brush or your fingers to separate and lift the hair?" Watching her reflection as inscrutably as she watched his, his eyes lingered on her mouth. "Brush," he said softly, the low gravelly sound rippling across her skin.

Running her hands through his hair, she asked, "Do you like a styled look or something more carefree?"

His face lit up in a devastating smile, pleasantly craggy lines appearing at the corners of his mouth and his eyes. "Messy suits me just fine."

She grinned, amused by the mischievous gleam in his eyes. "Is the wave natural or have you had your hair permed?" She combed the hair straight back from his forehead, studying the slightly rectangular shape of his face, his thin, straight nose, wide-set eyes and gently angled chin. To best complement his bone structure, she knew his hair should be brushed away from his face at the sides, his bangs left medium long and layered for fullness and manageability.

He seemed marginally irritated that she had even asked about a perm. "It's naturally wavy." He shifted, flexing his shoulders, tapping the soles of his boots against the tile.

"Do you part it on the side?" His hair showed no signs of thinning, she noted. No doubt the man would have a full glorious head of hair until he was eighty. And when he eventually grayed, his hair would be silvery, streaked with varying shades of gold. It would still be soft, flattering to the fair ivory-beige tone of his skin.

"Yes."

"Do you want to keep it that way?" Her question was reflective as she reached for her shears. His gaze narrowed, indicating that he didn't quite trust her judgment as a stylist, which, all factors considered, was probably as it should have been. She knew how she felt whenever she let someone new work on her hair.

"Yes." This time his tone was more clipped.

She suppressed a droll smile. "Okay." Her mind solely on her work once more, determined to prove his initial trust was justified, Colleen began by combing his hair down onto his forehead and adjusting the length of his bangs to just below the brow. In an effort to relax him she asked conversationally, "What and why are you filming here in Columbus? Or shouldn't I ask?"

"Not at all. I'm filming a teenage comedy and we needed a midwestern location. This is it."

Colleen snipped the hair at the back of his neck. She checked to make certain the layers of his hair were the correct length for his face shape, then decided to go a quarter inch shorter and resumed cutting. She gestured toward the mirror. "I cut your bangs to just slightly below your eyebrows. If they don't seem short enough after they've dried, we'll adjust them."

He glanced in the mirror and smiled approvingly. "Looks great so far."

"Well, stop me if you think I'm doing anything out of the ordinary or going too short on these layers."

"I will."

She worked in silence for a few moments, aware of Lyon's gaze riveted admiringly upon her. "Just out of curiosity, why didn't you have one of the stylists on the set do this? It probably would have been easier—cheaper, too."

For a split second his mouth dropped and he looked completely at a loss.

"The idea didn't occur to you?" she asked, amazed.

"No, as a matter of fact, it didn't. I guess it should have, though." He rubbed his fist on the seam of his jeans. His cheeks colored slightly and his mouth twisted to hide a sheepish grin.

She decided Lyon was like the proverbial absent-minded professor, at least where his haircuts were concerned. It was a humanizing trait and an oddly endearing one. "What do you usually do when you're filming on location?"

"To be truthful I usually just let it go until I get back to L.A. When I'm making a film, the last thing I'm concerned about is the state of my hair."

"What prompted you to get a haircut this time?"

He straightened until the small of his back was pressed firmly against his chair, his feet squarely on the floor. "The wind was blowing my hair into my eyes. Nearly blinded me when we were trying to shoot last week, despite my hat."

She was nearly finished. While waiting for him to get comfortable again, she glanced back at the silky damp-dry fringe of hair lying across his forehead.

"Since it's been bothering you, do you think that we ought to go a little shorter here?"

He agreed quickly, barely pausing to consult the mirror. "Yeah." They were both silent as she shortened his bangs another quarter inch. "How long have you been a stylist?" he asked.

"About eight years." Routinely she checked the layers of his hair for symmetry and length, in no hurry to be finished.

"Was it a lifetime ambition of yours?"

"Yes. I've always been fascinated with the difference a good cut can make in the way a person looks. To me it's an art." She trimmed his sideburns with a battery-operated razor she'd removed from her bag, then paid similar attention to the light feathering hair at the very nape of his neck.

"You mentioned you have guardianship of your younger sister. Do you work full-time?"

"I have to in order to support us." Colleen smiled. "Up until last year I had a housekeeper to help out, but when Amy turned sixteen she convinced me we didn't need her any longer. Since our insurance money had run out anyway, I capitulated. So now it is just the two of us again, and I have to admit we've been doing fine. Amy's a very reliable, trustworthy young woman."

"Has it always been just the two of you, since your parents died?"

"I've never been married if that's what you mean."

"Engaged?"

"No." In fact Amy vowed that Colleen would end up being a spinster. "I won't deny that there were times when I wished I had someone to help me with Amy," she continued, encouraged by Lyon's interested, understanding glance. "I am, after all, only her sister, with no experience in mothering. I've often felt at a loss. But somehow we've managed. And she's grown up all right." A fact Colleen credited largely to her move back to the Midwest and the solid, stable life-style she had established for them both.

"It must have been hard on you, giving up your own life to raise your sister," he observed.

What life, Colleen wondered. Aside from her career and a myriad of mostly casual friendships, there had been nothing to keep her in New York.

"Harder on her than on me, I'm afraid. Sometimes I..."

"What?" he prompted when she didn't continue.

"I just wish she weren't so...impetuous." Colleen sighed. How long had it been since anyone had ever listened to her so attentively? Had she ever confided so much about herself to anyone, so swiftly? She knew she hadn't. "Amy's hell-bent on becoming an actress and won't let anything stand in her way. I wanted her to have more of a childhood before becoming serious about a career."

"But she wants to work," he ascertained.

"Yes."

"She sounds like very few of the teenagers I've come in contact with, but many of the actresses I know," he observed, swiveling around to face her. "If that's what she wants to do in life, you should be proud of her."

"I am. At any rate I've tried to encourage her art. She's enrolled here in a special school for the performing arts, and she's active in community theatre."

He looked intrigued at the revelation rather than bored as she'd half expected him to be. "I didn't realize Columbus had that type of high school," he murmured. Thoughtfully he asked, "Do the two of you look alike?"

"We have the same color eyes, face shape, we're both blondes, though her hair is longer—to her waist. She claims it gives her more versatility as an actress." Colleen smiled, recalling all the times she had tried to get her sister to do even the slightest bit more than trim her tresses.

"Won't let you cut it, hmm?" Lyon guessed with a commiserating grin.

"Screams bloody murder every time I get near her with the scissors."

He laughed. "She'll grow out of it, but Amy is right. As an actress, long hair is a plus. It does give her more versatility in roles, especially period pieces, and wigs have their drawbacks."

Reaching for the hair dryer, she plugged it in and flicked it on. "Forgive me if I don't tell Amy you approve?" she teased.

Using both her fingers and a brush, she blow-dried his hair and then combed it into place. When she'd finished he stood and removed the towel from his shoulders.

Checking his reflection in the mirror, he ran a hand through his hair, nodding with satisfaction when every hair fell neatly and obediently back into place. "You did a nice job. Thanks, Colleen."

Impulsively she reached up to brush off a speck of hair stuck to his cheek. The brief contact surprised them both and she looked away in confusion. Glancing at the untidy mass of wheat-gold clippings that littered the floor, she fought the irrational urge to pick up a lock and take it home with her as a memento of the day.

Beside her, Lyon had shrugged into his shirt. Buttoning it quickly he tucked the hem into his jeans.

"I'll have housekeeping send up a maid to vacuum," she said, hurriedly packing her equipment.

He reached into his pocket and withdrew his wallet. "How much do I owe you?" Abruptly, he too was solemn and ill at ease.

She named the appropriate amount, sorry the appointment had to end. But now that it was over, she was anxious to be on her way.

He swiftly counted out the bills, adding a generous tip, then held her jacket while she slipped into it. His hands lingered briefly on her shoulders and at the warmth of his touch she longed to relax against him—to forget he was a client just for a second. But such an act would destroy her credibility as a professional, and she'd fought too hard for it to let her reputation be destroyed by a moment's impulsiveness. Like it or not, she still had Amy and herself to support.

Straightening determinedly, she slung her tote over her shoulder. Lyon led the way to the front door of the suite, then stopped, a hand on either side of the threshold, blocking her exit. His eyes met hers and the pulse began throbbing in her throat. He was so close she could feel the heat of his body, the warm soft whisper of his breath. His posture relaxed slightly as he stood there and he seemed unwilling to let her go. She found herself wanting to take and taste his lips—they were so close to her own. But it was he who broke the heart-stopping silence between them with his deep, throaty voice. "If you're not doing anything this evening, I'd like to take you out."

2

FOR A SECOND Colleen was so astonished she could
barely think, never mind form a coherent reply. She
struggled against the warm blush staining her cheeks
and words of indecision welled up in her tight throat
as he waited patiently for her answer. Never before
had she wanted so much to accept an invitation.
Lyon was any woman's dream come true. He was
handsome, successful and remarkably approacha-
ble, at least in private, for a man of his position. But
he was also an internationally renowned film director. Beyond the fact that she'd cut his hair, they had
nothing in common—nothing that would sustain
their friendship past a casual fling or his brief time
spent in Columbus. Yes, he wanted her company
now, when he was far away from home. But what
about tomorrow or the day after? As enamored as
she already was of him, she was hesitant to risk getting further involved. She didn't want to be anyone's one-night stand or small-city diversion.

Lyon shut the door partway, as if to block her escape, and continued convincingly, "I realize you
probably don't date clients, and I think that's a sound

policy. I rarely mix business and pleasure, either, but in this case I hope you'll make an exception to the rule." His gaze skimmed her face and throat, lingering briefly on her mouth before moving back to her eyes with a beseeching look that stole her breath away. "At least consider the possibility? Don't turn me down before you've thought about it," he whispered.

At his coaxing tone, her defenses slipped away, leaving her feeling vulnerable. From the moment they'd met she'd been achingly aware of him. The casual way he'd shucked his shirt, and later drawn it back on, had riveted her attention to the smooth muscles of his arms and chest. As she'd worked on his hair, she'd observed the inherent gentleness in his relaxed face. It had gone straight to her heart. And standing so close to him, then and now, she was pleasurably inundated by his clean, uniquely male scent.

During the time she'd been in the suite, the task of cutting his hair to his satisfaction had kept her distracted and remote, at least for part of the time. Now that she was ready to leave she had no such protective preoccupation. She was more mesmerized by him than ever.

"I'm only going to be in Columbus for three weeks." Shutting the door completely, he leaned against it and waited, regarding her steadily all the while.

Clearly he didn't want to waste any time. Colleen hesitated, "It's a very tempting offer but—"

He cut off her protest. "I'll have you home early, I promise. You can show me the sights."

She couldn't think coherently when he looked at her. She turned toward the windows. He moved, almost reflexively, to close the distance between them, his steps inaudible on the carpet. Hands lightly gripping her shoulders, he turned her to face him.

"I want to talk to someone I don't work with on the set, someone who is not enthralled with my celebrity status. I'm not out to hurt you, Colleen," he stressed quietly. His grasp relaxed slightly as her body became more pliant under his firm but compellingly gentle touch. "I just want some sane conversation, a normal evening between two friends. Or—" his gaze deepened desirously, then lightened, as if he'd suddenly realized he was being too presumptuous "—two people who could be friends."

She knew how he felt. A normal evening between two adults did sound enticing. Never could she remember being this strongly and swiftly attracted to any man. On impulse she tossed her normal reserve aside. "I'll have to phone my sister," she cautioned. "Let her know I'll be out late."

"Fine."

Colleen couldn't shake the impression he was capturing everything about her in his mind, preserving it as surely as he harbored moments on film.

He went on studying her while she dialed the desk for an outside line, then finally excused himself and disappeared into the bedroom. But even though she was still slightly nervous and on edge with this man, the prospect of the pleasurable evening ahead made her smile.

Amy wasn't home so Colleen left a message on the answering machine, telling her not to wait dinner, that she'd be late because she had a last-minute date.

Lyon came back into the room just as she completed her call. "I couldn't help but overhear part of that," he remarked. "Trouble locating your sister?"

"I'd forgotten she has a rehearsal at the community theatre until nine o'clock."

"No date for her either on a Friday night? That much dedication is unusual in one so young." Lyon looked thoughtful, though his tone had been teasing.

Colleen shook her head in bemusement, adding in the same light tone, "That's what I keep telling her." More honestly still, she admitted, "I worry her life is too narrow."

"Is she happy acting?" he countered.

"Supremely."

He shrugged. "Then why worry about it?"

Colleen wondered. Maybe she was being overpossessive.

Lyon continued, "Her dedication is not all that unusual, not if she's serious about her craft." He seemed to be genuinely interested in everything about Colleen, including her travails with her sister.

"She is."

He was silent for a moment, thinking, then asked, "Is she any good?"

"Yes, in my thoroughly unprejudiced opinion." Colleen laughed lightly and glanced heavenward. "Her reviews from the local critics have been consistently favorable and she's been approached by Northwestern University about a scholarship next summer, if her grades and entrance-exam scores are good enough."

Again he looked pensive. Finally he murmured, "I'd like to meet her sometime."

Colleen was unsure of whether he was just saying that to be polite or if he really meant it; he still seemed to be deep in thought. "I'm sure that can be arranged, knowing Amy."

He nodded, but said nothing more, so she let the subject drop. Tilting her head to the side, she looked up at him. "Where did you want to go?"

He shrugged and smiled down at her once again. "You're the expert on local pastimes. What would you suggest? I've got a rental car in the hotel garage, so transportation is no problem."

She took refuge in the role of tour guide. "Most of the museums here are closed at night. The community theatre is still in rehearsal for their next play—

performances won't begin for another week. The symphony orchestra has the night off."

He was watching her closely. "I'd just as soon stay out of the tourist traps," he admitted. "To be honest, it would be refreshing just to spend an evening doing what everyone else in Columbus does."

Colleen thought for a moment. "Football games are very popular here. Unfortunately, Ohio State doesn't play until tomorrow."

"What about the high schools? Don't they play?" Not waiting for a reply, he disappeared into the bedroom. When he emerged a second later, he had the softest cashmere sweater she had ever seen crumpled in one hand. While she watched he pulled the beige V-neck garment over his head. The subdued sandy color emphasized the golden highlights in his hair.

Her mouth was dry as she picked up on their conversation. "Well, yes, but..."

Casually he adjusted the sweater. "Don't you have some school you'd like to see? An old alma mater or a favorite team?"

She blushed slightly, clearing her throat. So the man was still dressing, getting ready to go out. She didn't have to gape. "As a matter of fact, Arlington Heights, my old high school, is playing the local Catholic-school team tonight." Though Amy looked down her nose at organized sports, Colleen loved the high-spirited fanfare.

"Big rivalry, hmm?" he teased. "Private versus public schools?"

"Right. How did you—"

"I come from a family of five children. My parents are Catholic, and we attended the local parochial schools from elementary on up. I played on the team you probably would have facetiously sung verbally fractured hymns to."

She blushed riotously. "You've got me pegged. My friends and I were a pretty pagan lot."

"Well, don't worry, I won't embarrass you by cheering for the rival team. Though I might be tempted to, for old time's sake."

"Well, don't sit on Arlington's side if you do. You might be mobbed," she advised with an exaggerated narrowed glance.

"Point well taken. I'll control myself. What time does the game start?"

Without warning he strode closer.

Colleen's heart started ticking at breakneck speed, and she had to battle the urge to melt into him then and there. "Umm...seven-thirty or eight o'clock, I think." One step closer and she'd be able to touch his shoulder, brush the softness of his sweater with her cheek. With a start she realized she was acting like some sort of groupie. No doubt the man had had enough of that.

He glanced at his watch, noting it was almost seven o'clock. "Then we'd better get going. Unless you need to go home first?"

She pictured her stylish condominium with its long living-room sofa and comfortable bed. No, she didn't want to take Lyon there, not even for an instant. "My car's in the parking garage. I'll just pick it up later, when we come back to the hotel."

"It's okay with me if you're sure it's safe for you to drive home alone that late at night."

She was touched by his concern for her safety. "I live in a security-patrolled area. We have excellent law enforcement here, so it's no problem." She turned to watch him as he stepped past her and reached for the dun leather jacket draped over the back of one chair. He rifled through it for his room key and deposited it into the pocket of his pants.

"You're sure you don't mind going to a high-school game?" The disconcerting thought that this was no way to entertain a celebrity had just struck her.

"Not at all. It'll be fun." Lyon felt his back pocket for his wallet, threw a soft ivory cashmere scarf around his neck and stuffed leather driving gloves into the pockets of his aviator-style jacket. "Besides that—" he shot her a warning glance as if to clue her in on what she might be leaving herself open for "— if we went anywhere posh or the least bit trendy, there's the possibility I might be recognized and descended upon for autographs."

Colleen had been so involved in her quandary over whether to accept his invitation or not, she'd completely overlooked such a problem. Admittedly, she didn't go out of her way to keep up with celebrity news, but there were plenty of others who did. And since the debut of his first movie five years ago, Lyon's photo had often been displayed in the fan magazines the salon carried for teens.

Now she did have reservations. As much as she had been looking forward to going out with him, she didn't want to be caught in the middle of a hungry mob.

His shoulders slumped as he took in her apprehensive expression. "I guess I shouldn't have mentioned the publicity problem or the potential of it, no matter how unlikely it might prove to be here in Columbus. But I didn't want you to think we were hanging out in an out-of-the-way place because I was a tightwad." He flashed a quick grin. "Or worse—afraid to be seen publicly with you."

She never would have thought that of him. He'd been such a gentleman thus far. "I must admit, I'm not wild about being the only object standing between you and your adoring public," she joked at last. "But I think I can handle it." At least she hoped she could. And she did want to be with him. That much became clearer with every passing moment.

"All right," he said softly, taking her arm in his. "But for the record, I don't think there will be any

problem. As I said, I only arrived in Columbus today. Aside from a few officials and the hotel person-
nel, no one knows I'm here. I always like to keep as
low a profile as possible, for as long as possible,
wherever I'm working."

Which, knowing how famous the man was,
would be the case only as long as his presence went
unreported.

On the journey down, the elevator was crowded
with a late-embarking group of partying conven-
tioners. The group was all male, and it was clear
from the slightly stale, bittersweet stench of liquor,
too-bright stares and flushed faces that most of them
had been drinking heavily. Being the only woman
in the elevator, Colleen instantly felt threatened just
by virtue of her sex. As unobtrusively as possible,
she nudged closer to Lyon. He reacted by putting a
possessive arm around her waist. Every line in his
body became hard and threatening. There could
have been no question in anyone's mind that she was
well and devotedly protected by him. Nonetheless,
Colleen breathed a sigh of relief when the elevator
finally reached the lobby and they all got off.

"Thanks for looking fierce," she murmured as
Lyon released his grip on her waist.

"I was glad to do it." Cupping his hand under her
elbow, he guided her through the lobby.

Behind the reception desk the reservations clerk
registered a look of shock, and Colleen flushed self-

consciously, realizing it must look as if she'd picked up a customer. Nevertheless it felt wonderful to be with Lyon. He stopped at the desk long enough to ask that his phone messages be taken for him, then continued toward the exit.

Colleen shifted the equipment bag over to her left shoulder as they moved through the revolving door. Lyon slanted her a concerned look. "Is that bag hurting your shoulder?" Outside, a crisp breeze stirred the air. The surrounding granite, marble and glass skyscrapers were bathed in a dusky glow of early evening.

"It does get heavy after a while," she admitted.

"Here, let me carry it for you." Without missing a beat he switched the bag from her left shoulder to his right. His hand still hooked around her elbow, he led her toward the parking garage across the street. They took his car, a black Mazda RX-7, to the Arlington High-Sisters of Charity game, deciding to eat later, rather than miss the kickoff. Colleen gave directions, pointing out the Ohio State University campus and the Ohio State School for the Blind as they drove.

"What about the Center of Science and Industry? Have you been there?"

Laughing, she teased, "You have been reading your tour guides!"

He half suppressed a self-conscious grin. "I always like to know as much as possible about the area where I'm filming," he replied. "Must be a holdover from the days when I scouted locations for one of the studios. I did it summers to earn my college tuition," he added in response to her inquiring look. "The experience taught me a lot, though I can't say it did as much for my employers. They rarely even read my reports, let alone looked at any of the dazzling photos I turned in. Or so it seemed at the time."

Colleen laughed. "I guess you've gotten your best revenge."

He shot her an amused glance. "Maybe I have at that."

The stadium was already filling by the time they parked the car and approached the gates. Used to going dutch treat with her casual male friends, Colleen reached for the clasp on her handbag as they approached the ticket booth saying, "I'll spring for the tickets."

"No," he refused adamantly, staying her hand with the warm clasp of his own, "this evening is my treat."

She grinned. "Just remember I offered."

"I don't think I'll soon forget."

Although it was not yet dark, the stadium lights overhead gleamed brightly. Excited shouts of students and the animated conversation of spectators waiting in line competed with the discordant sounds of rival high-school marching bands tuning up. Vibrant young girls in cheerleader uniforms dashed past, their swishing red-and-white shakers held tightly in their fists. A similarly clad group in green-and-yellow uniforms followed soon after. Colleen sighed wistfully.

"What is it?" Lyon asked.

"I was just wishing Amy was here tonight to enjoy the fun or that the performing-arts high school had a team of its own—sports events to attend."

"The lure of greasepaint has its own rewards," he responded, and Colleen reminded herself that he used children under eighteen for leading parts in many of his films. "I'm sorry," she apologized falteringly. "I didn't mean to imply. . ."

"That's all right. You sound like a stage mother, and considering your special relationship with your sister, that's neither unexpected nor unwarranted. You never have to apologize for loving someone, Colleen, or wanting only what's best for them."

"Thanks for understanding." She truly appreciated his sensitivity.

The smell of popcorn and hot chocolate permeated the crisp, clean October-evening air. "Sure brings back the memories, doesn't it?" Lyon commented as they made their way through the gates and selected a seat near the top section of the bleachers.

Colleen nodded. "Especially the scent of aftershave and perfume! I think every brand known to man must be represented somewhere here tonight."

It was a fragrant, almost overpowering flowery-spicy mix.

He nodded and grinned. "I know what you mean. I think every student we passed has had a liberal dousing of some artificial scent before he or she arrived."

Most of the girls were decked out in twisted beads of various colors with matching bracelets and pierced earrings. Though jeans and oxford-cloth shirts predominated beneath the Arlington High jackets, there was a smattering of trendy parachute pants, silk shirts and spangled T-shirts.

Colleen and Lyon watched a cluster of boys carefully comb their hair before moving to sit next to a group of girls. "I guess there are worse things for them to be into than grooming fixations. And their not-so-latent attraction to the opposite sex."

"Amen to that." He squeezed her hand.

She was momentarily transported back to the less-demanding time of her own high-school days. "How simple the requirements for happiness."

Lyon's body was warm beside hers in the chilling night air, his voice was a rough seductive whisper, inviting confession. "What did you yearn for then?"

She blushed beet red, unable to tell him anything other than the truth. "I was a hopeless romantic. I dreamed of marriage, children, a satisfying career, too—but mostly the personal things. Have you ever been married?" she asked impulsively, hoping to shift the conversation back onto his turf.

"Yes. I was. We were divorced several years ago." He looked away, as if the memory disturbed him still.

"I'm sorry," she said softly, compassionately.

He reached over and squeezed her hand. "Did you spend all four years at Arlington High?" he asked casually after the pregame show ended and the playing began.

"Only the first year and a half," she replied distractedly, her attention riveted on the field. She watched in dismay as the rival team captured the ball, then ran it back to their own forty-yard line.

"Where'd you go after that?" Lyon signaled a vendor and after ascertaining her preference, purchased them each a cup of steaming cocoa.

"To a private school in Washington, D.C. My dad was in politics, a member of the state senate while I was young. Later, when I was in high school, he ran for a position in Congress. He was a United States senator at the time of his death."

Lyon looked stricken. "I'm sorry. I didn't realize..."

"That's okay. I wouldn't have expected you to keep up with Ohio politics. I often wonder, though, what Dad might have been able to accomplish had his life not been ended so suddenly."

The sudden fierce roaring of the crowd prevented her from having to continue the painful conversation. Lyon half rose from his seat as Arlington High made a spectacular pass. The crowd screamed and cheered. Within seconds the band had jubilantly struck up the fight song.

"How did you like living in Washington?" Lyon asked after resuming his seat. Though the question sounded innocent enough, Colleen felt as if he was trying to gauge how well she adapted to change.

"It was a difficult transition at first, simply because I was in high school and I'd left so many friends behind in Columbus. But my parents kept the family farm here, north of the city, and we made frequent visits, so Dad could keep in touch with his constituents. That made it easier. And as I told you earlier, I did come back, and went to City College with the rest of my friends. If anything was difficult, it was the increased scrutiny the press gave us in Washington. I found that...dismaying at times—an intrusion."

Before he could ask anything else, the opposing team regained possession of the ball by intercepting a pass and ran fifty-two yards to make the first touchdown of the evening. Lyon and she exchanged dismal glances as the opposing team celebrated with a deafening rendition of their fight song. He moved closer, sliding an arm around her waist. His touch stirred her senses, giving her a good indication of just

how masterful a lover he would be. When...and if.
She had to stop thinking this way! She had to remember who he was, remind herself that soon he
would be leaving. His free hand reached out to cover
hers while the hand on her waist tightened, too. His
warm breath stirred her hair, whispering across her
cheek.

With great effort she spoke casually, "Where did
you go to school?"

"Los Angeles."

Aware of the other people around them, she asked
carefully, in a soft curious tone, "Did you always
know what your career would be?"

"I knew what I wanted to do." Lyon lifted his hand
from hers and rubbed absentmindedly at a well-
worn patch on his jeans directly above his knee. "I
went to UCLA, studied hard and made use of every
connection I had. My father was a sound technician
for a major studio," he explained. "So that gave me
some entry into the field."

His real success, Colleen knew from the limited
reading she'd done on him, Lyon had achieved completely on his own.

"Hey!" A youthful male voice interrupted unexpectedly. A tall, lanky teenage boy and a chubby
bespectacled friend clambered boisterously over the
bleachers in front of them, pushing other spectators
aside, staring adoringly up at Lyon all the while.

Colleen's heart sank as she realized what was about to happen.

"I told you it was him! Lyon! Lyon Haggerty!" The tall boy waved vigorously. "Hey, it is you, isn't it?"

To Lyon's chagrin, the boy crowed triumphantly to the crowd around him, "I knew it was him all the time! Nobody else believed me, but *I* knew...."

Removing his hand from her waist, Lyon rose easily, graciously but reluctantly taking the hand the young boy offered as he scrambled closer, stumbling over spectators and bleachers. Within seconds more people were pushing forward. Programs were being introduced for signature, girls were upending their purses looking for pens.

"Colleen." Lyon grabbed her hand, grasped it briefly. He seemed to be asking her to stay with him and weather the crowd.

Colleen glanced down and saw a young man with a Nikon slung around his neck standing at the bottom row of the bleachers, his quizzical regard focused on them. When he lifted his camera and started clicking, she groaned inwardly.

"Lyon—" her hand on his arm, she leaned forward to whisper in his ear "—I'll meet you by the front gate. Whenever you can get away."

Before he had a chance to reply another adoring fan had pushed between them. "Just one autograph, Mr. Haggerty, please." A little girl in pigtails, designer jeans, T-shirt and Arlington Elementary jacket smiled up at him. "I've seen every one of your movies and so have all my older brothers."

A person would have had to be heartless to refuse the child's request. Lyon wasn't. He was obviously upset about the intrusion, but there was nothing either of them could do except grin and bear it. At the very least, he owed it to his fans to be gracious, and as his date, Colleen felt she owed it to him to understand.

Trust me, her look said, *I know what I'm doing.* She had been in the same situation many times before with her father.

He shot her a helpless look, shrugged and bent to answer a question from a teenage boy at his side. Yet another person pushed between Colleen and Lyon, then another and another. The football game was all but forgotten; she moved lithely, watching as the spectators became progressively less polite as the numbers surrounding Lyon increased. Even people who seemed to have little idea what the commotion was about were rising and moving in the direction of the fray. So much for trying to keep a low profile, Colleen thought, as Lyon was obscured from her sight.

Colleen began her descent, taking the steps with ease, reaching the grassy embankment below, slipping behind the tiered seats, through the crowd, past the refreshment stands and rest rooms, heading in the direction of the gate. Ten minutes later she was still waiting there. She began to wonder if he had misunderstood where she had intended to meet him and was about to head off in the direction of his parked car when she heard someone call her name.

She turned to see Lyon jogging toward her. His stride was measured and swift, his face etched with concern for her welfare. He'd pulled up the collar of his jacket but he was still readily identifiable to anyone who knew he'd been there at the game. His eyes were glittering with barely suppressed excitement, and she knew he'd enjoyed what must have been a very difficult escape.

She looked past him uneasily, hardly able to believe he hadn't been followed. There were no spectators trailing along behind him, indeed no one but a lone security guard was in the immediate vicinity, but she knew better than to think they were home free.

As though sharing her thoughts, Lyon took her by the hand and led her through the gate past several columns of vehicles, only then pausing in the shelter of a dark-blue van. She looked up into his face. "How'd you get out?" she asked breathlessly.

"Luck and ingenuity," he informed her with a wink. "In case you didn't notice all that screaming and yelling a moment ago, Arlington High just scored their first touchdown of the evening. I think they even made the extra point, too. I slipped away when everyone else turned to watch the play. Used an old stuntman's trick and dropped over the side of the bleachers and sort of catwalked my way down to the ground."

It sounded dangerous. He looked exhilarated. His physical agility and quick thinking impressed her. She smiled. "I'm surprised no one tried to follow you."

His expression turned serious. "I'm glad they didn't." Linking his arm with hers, he began walking in the direction of his car.

"You were wonderful just now, you know that?" He stopped so abruptly she walked right into him, her cheek brushing the soft cool surface of the jacket he wore over the solidness of his shoulder. His eyes glittered with admiration, desire. She found herself suddenly weak-kneed, wanting only more closeness between them, afraid of her own desire.

The night had grown cooler during the past hour. She found herself shivering in the wintry breeze. Her hands cupping opposite elbows, she hugged herself fiercely, but the effort to protect herself from her own impulsive yearnings for further intimacy failed. His regard gentled. He lifted his hand to her face and brushed his knuckles ever so lightly across the line of her chin. "I'm sorry if that was a bother for you," he apologized softly. "Honestly, I didn't think I would be recognized there tonight; if I had, I wouldn't have asked you to go."

He gently tilted her face up to his, his thumb brushing from cheekbone to jaw, lingering near her mouth. Another shiver went through her, this one generated by sheer passion. "Tell me you're not angry with me," he whispered. From the intent way he looked at her, she knew he really cared how she felt.

"No, of course I'm not angry."

His hands dropped to rest lightly on her shoulders. He studied her wordlessly and the intensity in his dark gaze inflamed her senses even more. His nearness threatening to overwhelm her, she swayed against him, rested a hand flat against his chest and took a deep steadying breath. In the distance, the roaring of the crowd faded, drifted away to nothingness. They both glanced up in the direction of the stadium lights and saw from the scoreboard that the first half of the football game had come to an end. The marching bands were lining up on either side of the field—halftime.

"We'd better get out of here," Lyon decided abruptly, capturing her hand.

Neither of them wanted another scene with his fans, so they hurried to the car, Colleen still shivering with every rapid step. Lyon unlocked the car and ushered her in.

"Still cold?" He turned to face her as the car was warming up.

"Not so much," she lied through chattering teeth. If she'd been aware of him before, in his hotel suite, and later standing so close to him in the open star-studded night, she was even more overwhelmed by his presence now. She found herself longing to touch him, to reach out and capture his hand. Fearing he might interpret such a gesture as a groupielike come-on, she did nothing.

"Sorry we didn't get to see the end of the game?" Lyon asked, shifting the car into gear. It lurched out of the parking space and bumped over the uneven grounds.

"No." Just sorry our date had to end, she added silently.

"The score was tied 7-7."

"There will be other gridiron clashes." She clasped her hands together in an effort to warm them and sandwiched them between her thighs. There wouldn't be another date with Lyon.

"Want to get something to eat?" he asked abruptly. "It's still early."

"After what just happened?" she asked incredulously. She was stunned that he would even consider risking his privacy again.

"Surely you must know some place we could go where we wouldn't be bothered." He halted the car at a stop sign and turned to look at her, sliding his arm along the back of the seat. The near contact combined with his determined look undid her. She wet her lips uncertainly and his arm slid down to touch and capture a strand of her hair. She watched as he curled the silken end around his finger. "I want to be with you, Colleen," he said softly.

And she wanted to be with him. She cleared her throat nervously. "There's a family-owned pizza place about halfway between here and the hotel. It's not sophisticated." And was hardly the sort of place in which to entertain such a celebrated man.

His expressive eyes sparkled. "How's their pizza?"

"First-rate. Don't expect tablecloths or china, though," she warned.

"Who needs them?"

Minutes later they were pulling into the parking lot. Located in a largely residential area, the twenty-year-old establishment was housed in a small square building. The only indication that it was a restaurant rather than a private residence was a small pink-and-blue neon sign above the door. Inside, the family-style restaurant was deserted except for a harried woman with two little boys and an elderly couple. After the football game, Colleen knew business would pick up tenfold.

Because it was essentially a wait-on-yourself establishment, Colleen stopped at the register where she and Lyon consulted the menu printed on the wall. Concluding they were both starved, they ordered a large pizza with everything. Picking up two mugs of root beer on the way, they walked over to a worn vinyl booth at the far end of the establishment and settled in across from each other.

"You really love football, don't you?" Lyon asked, unwrapping the paper from his straw and sliding it into his drink.

"Yes." She smiled and took a sip of her root beer. His gaze focused on the movement and her heartbeat quickened in response. "Did you play team sports?"

"Football, basketball. I was on the track team, too."

No wonder he'd looked so athletically capable running out of the stadium, she thought. "Are you a jogger?"

"At home, yes. I usually do five miles about three times a week. When I'm on the road filming, it's not always possible due to weather conditions, then I substitute racquetball."

A call from the front counter indicated their pizza was ready and Lyon walked up to get it. The waitress, a plump and pretty girl in her late teens could barely take her eyes off Lyon's face. Whether or not she recognized him as the Hollywood Haggerty, Colleen couldn't tell.

"So, how's work on your new picture going?" Colleen asked once he'd returned and they'd begun to eat.

"Overall, very well, although so far we've done mostly studio work. To complicate matters, one of the actresses I had signed bowed out of her contract for health reasons. Poor kid has mononucleosis." He shook his head sympathetically. "I haven't been able to replace her yet and we're supposed to be filming that segment next week. Her doctor says there's no way she can continue work on this film. And I agree she shouldn't jeopardize her health. Unfortunately, no one the casting agency in Los Angeles has come up with seems right for the part. I'm going to be interviewing some actresses from Chicago and New York tomorrow. Though from what I've already seen I'm not sure any of them will do, either. Nonetheless, I have to cast the role by Monday at the latest."

Fascinated, Colleen asked, "Precisely what are you looking for?"

He grinned. "Someone to play the mayor's daughter—the girl every guy for miles around is in love with, the type that can lead them all on a merry chase. She has to be spectacularly beautiful, intelligent, able to convincingly play the flirt, yet be vulnerable on screen when need be."

"Finding the right girl to play that part sounds like an impossible task," Colleen remarked.

He shrugged. "I know what I'm looking for. My main problem right now is time. There, I am in a bind." He frowned again, absorbed in thoughts of the task ahead of him. After a moment he glanced at her, his face full of that magic charm. "Am I boring you?" He watched her with cautious eyes.

"No." *Never.* She smiled shyly as his smile deepened. No doubt about it, this man could steal her heart in two seconds flat. During the rest of the meal he entertained her with stories of problems on past movies, and when at last they drove to the parking garage where she'd left her own metallic-blue Volkswagen, she hated to leave. Slinging her bag of equipment over her arm, she stepped out of his car while he held the door open.

"Thanks for a lovely evening." *One of the loveliest of my life,* she thought, feeling as foolishly worshipful of him as any adoring fan.

"You're welcome."

Hands shoved in the pockets of his jacket, he strolled with her to her car. The parking garage was devoid of people and silent except for the echoing sound of their shoes on the bare cement. The late-model cars of hotel guests gleamed under the bright fluorescent lights. Nervously Colleen turned up the collar of her coat against the cold. This was the moment she'd been dreading. It was all over and now he'd bid her a casual goodbye.

"I'd like to see you again," he stated, his voice very low.

A strand of hair blew across her face. Tenderly he brushed it aside and tucked it back behind her ear. The heartbeats stretched out between them. Colleen wanted to see him again, too, but she wasn't cut out for a speedy no-commitment romance, nor did she want to be just friends. The truth was she desired him and wanted him to desire her. But beyond that her thinking was hazy with indecision. His life was so far from Columbus and her mundane existence. "Lyon, I..."

As if reading her mind, he said softly, "I'm not just out for a quick roll in the hay."

"I know that." But her voice was thick and she couldn't meet his eyes.

"Do you? I wonder."

At his knowing tone, exasperation and anger swept through her; she couldn't suppress the fears and doubts crowding her mind. "Lyon, I worked in New York, remember? I know how most of the men in the film industry out there treat the women they meet." She'd heard plenty of horror stories from the actresses she'd worked on regularly. Casting couches seemed to be an accepted hazard of the trade in L.A.

Anger sharpened the planes of his face. A muscle clenched and unclenched along his jawline, but he didn't deny her assertion. "I'm not most men," he said gruffly.

She met his gaze straight on. "But you do have your pick of nearly the entire female race." At his dismissing hiss, she went on, "I'm not trying to give you a hard time. I'm just trying to be honest. I don't want to be hurt. Is that so bad?"

Apparently it wasn't. He clasped one of her hands and rubbed it between the two of his. "If you want to know the truth, I think you're succumbing to the old east coast, west coast rivalry. You should never believe even half of what you hear. I'd never make love to you and then discard you like yesterday's old news, Colleen. I wouldn't, couldn't, just walk away without a backward glance. People mean more to me than that. You mean more to me."

She believed him; his treatment of the crowd, total strangers, had proved that much to her.

Lyon sighed heavily. "I won't lie and say I don't want to make love to you. I do. I haven't thought of anything else since I first laid eyes on you."

His directness caught her off guard and she had to fight for breath. "We just met," she managed to sputter. A tingling sensation had started in her stomach and was moving lower with every moment that passed.

"Yes, we did," he agreed, encircling her waist with his hands, drawing her toward him. "And we're going to see each other again. And again. And again."

It was a statement she couldn't refute. The protest she would have voiced under any other circumstance was cut off by the slow descent of his mouth, the gentle touch of his fingertips beneath her chin. His lips brushed against hers lightly, infusing her with incredible warmth. It was October outside, and yet it was summer...flowers...softness.... When she didn't resist, his tongue glided past her lips, past her teeth, to sweep her mouth with voluptuous leisure. One kiss, and he had invoked her emotional surrender and a tiny groan of yearning escaped from deep within her.

What remained of Lyon's control expired. "Tell me this is real," he whispered raggedly against her mouth.

It was better than real; it was her every fantasy come true. "If it's a dream I don't ever want to wake up," she murmured, opening her eyes to drink in the sight of him. His face was flushed with the warmth of his desire, his eyes gentle, so gentle.

"Colleen," he shook his head in confusion. "You sweet, incredible..." Wonderingly, he caught her up against him. And then all was forgotten in the passion that bound them together. The loneliness and isolation of their pasts seemed so far away. His hands tangled in her hair, and a new, more potent yearning swept through her as his mouth moved languorously, deliberately over hers.

Colleen drew a shaky breath, moaning as he wedged closer and his legs pressed length to length against hers. The imprint of his desire was taut, demanding, all primitive-male ardor. Involuntarily she arched her hips into his, needing, wanting so much more.... And then her arms were around his neck, one of her hands combing through the curling softness of his wheat-gold hair, the other firmly against the broad plane of his shoulder. She wanted him so much she thought she would die. She felt the warmth of his chest as he deliberately grazed her breasts, and then he was pulling her even closer, whispering her name and deepening the kiss even more erotically. His tongue swept the sweet cavern of her mouth, drew back, then explored her mouth fervently again. She clung to him, returning kiss for kiss, not wanting it ever to end. And yet in the very back of her mind, she knew that it must—they were in a parking garage....

Eventually, when both were breathless and weak, he drew back, staring down at her with the same sleepy-eyed look he'd had earlier when she finished shampooing his hair. It was as if without rhyme or reason they had found themselves in the middle of a cyclone from which neither could escape easily or unscathed. A shaky breath escaped her parted lips. With the release from his arms came the shattering of her world.

"I'll call you," he promised. Wordlessly he opened her car door and lightly guided her into the driver's seat, then pivoted and stalked back to stand against his rented car.

With trembling hands circling the wheel, Colleen drove off. Several miles later she could still feel the burning imprint of his kisses. The sensation comforted and aroused simultaneously.

3

"So, CINDERELLA, HOW WAS YOUR DATE?" Amy didn't even wait for Colleen to close the door. She halted her sit-ups and locked her arms around her bent knees. Her shimmering waist-length hair was loosely braided and pulled to one side. She wore a pink-and-gray jogging suit and had been simultaneously going through the calisthenics she did every night and the lines from her latest play.

"Okay." Colleen tossed down her handbag. Steadying herself with one hand on the back of the sofa, she bent to take off her shoes. "No, more than okay," she amended lightheartedly. "It was fun." She smiled dreamily, feeling as if she were walking on air.

"Fun?" Amy's light brows rose another teasing notch as she looked her sister up and down. "Well, that's a first. Usually the men you drag in are 'interesting' or very 'goal oriented.' No one's ever been fun before! This one must be a contender for soul mate."

"Ho, ho." Colleen shot back dryly. But Amy was right. Most of the men she had dated recently were dull. "So what have you been up to? How was play practice?"

"Fine. We have our first dress rehearsal tomorrow morning. The first real performance is a week from tomorrow." She grinned. "Everyone's got the jitters."

"And you?" Colleen asked.

Amy shrugged nonchalantly. "I've got my part down pat."

"Confident, aren't you?"

Amy straightened her legs and bent forward rhythmically, doing a series of stretching exercises. "You know I'm a quick study." She frowned. "Some of the others aren't." Amy was always bored going over scenes again and again.

Colleen leaned against the couch, idly surveying the room. Their condominium was decorated in what both sisters whimsically termed "early garage sale." Wicker furniture, spray painted white and adorned with gaily patterned cushions, dominated the springlike yellow, green and white decor. There was an abundance of plants, plenty of books and magazines and stacks of trade magazines for Amy and periodicals on the art of cutting and styling hair for Colleen placed about the room. In addition dog-eared scripts littered every spare surface.

"Back to your date. Tell me more about this mystery man. Did you know it's almost one o'clock?" Amy rolled to one side and began doing scissor leg lifts. "You haven't stayed out that late in a long time."

Normally Colleen tried to be home evenings for Amy's sake, and when she did go out she was always in by eleven. She hesitated. "I'm sorry if you were worried. I guess I lost track of the time. I went to the Arlington High game tonight."

"I wasn't worried. I know you can take care of yourself. I am dying of curiosity! As for the hour, there was an old Kate Hepburn movie I wanted to see."

Colleen had the feeling her little sister sometimes saw as much as any mother. Maybe that was the secret to their close and loving relationship; they mothered each other as need be.

"Who won?"

"Won? Oh. . ." Colleen made a great show of clearing her throat. "Well, actually, we didn't stay to see all of the second half."

"Mmm-hmm." Her sister jumped quickly to conclusions. "So, who's the hunk? How, when, where and why did you meet him?"

"One question at a time, little sister." Colleen got a good look at herself in the mirror. No doubt about it, she had been thoroughly kissed. Her lipstick was gone, her hair was mussed. There was a warm glow in her cheeks, an enigmatic sparkle in her eyes that was impossible to hide from an inquisitive, hopelessly romantic and dramatically inclined younger sister. Colleen wished there was some way to break the news to Amy without getting a violent reaction, some way to make herself feel less foolishly love struck. "I went out with Lyon Haggerty."

Amy jumped lithely to her feet, looking totally incredulous. Both hands were planted squarely on her hips. "*The* Lyon Haggerty?"

"One and the same." Colleen raked a hand through her hair, watching the tendrils fall through her spread fingers like splinters of spun silver and gold.

A myriad of expressions from disbelieving to dreamy crossed Amy's face as she danced closer. She bent over, searching Colleen's face. "You're putting me on!" They both knew the joke would have been a cruel one, as enamored as Amy was of all things theatrical.

"No, I'm not." Amy's passionate interest was precisely what Colleen had been hoping to avoid.

"For heaven's sake, don't be so closemouthed! Where'd you meet him?" Amy followed a suddenly restless Colleen out to the kitchen, watching as her sister removed a container from the refrigerator and poured herself a tall glass of grapefruit juice.

Colleen felt herself flush slightly as she recounted the meeting. "At the Regency Hotel's penthouse suite. I cut his hair this afternoon."

"And didn't call me?" Amy asked, amazed and slightly put out.

"I *did* call."

"That message you left on the recorder didn't say with whom you had a date! Honestly, Colleen, the very least you could have done was brought the man home to meet me."

With more care than necessary Colleen returned the pitcher to the refrigerator. She didn't want to see her sister nurture unrealistic expectations. "He's in town to shoot location scenes for his new movie, Amy."

Amy mulled that over for a minute. "Does he need any extras?"

"I didn't ask." She debated silently, wondering whether to tell Amy that Lyon was looking for someone to play the part of the mayor's daughter.

Amy groaned, cradling her head in both palms. "Honestly, sometimes I can't believe we're related!" She paused. Her head shot up to reveal glittering blue-gray eyes. "You're going to see him again, aren't you?" She seemed to be fervently praying for just that.

Colleen blushed in response. She shot her sister a glance of exaggerated impatience, hoping to quell Amy's penchant for questions. "You've been seeing too many movies." Secretly, though, Colleen was pleased. Was it that obvious that she was full of giddy excitement? She took her sister by the shoulders and peered down at her. "Listen to me. You've got to promise me you won't do anything foolish, like trying to get in to see Lyon." Maybe if she tried hard enough, she could get Amy an audition.

Amy drew an X between her breasts. "Cross my heart, I promise I won't storm his hotel." She rubbed her hands together and grinned impishly. "So when's he coming over? How about asking him to dinner tomorrow?" She reached behind her in the rack for a cookbook. "Maybe there's a way we can work a little Lady Macbeth into quiche."

Colleen placed a staying hand on her arm, not entirely sure her sister was joking. "Amy, I know this is exciting. But let's not get carried away. Even if Lyon did 'discover' you, you still have to finish high school."

Amy sighed. At seventeen she had savvy and was sophisticated and determined. She'd been robbed of her youth and the opportunity to be carefree by their parents' death. But in spite of all that she was still remarkably innocent in some respects. "Did you tell Lyon your sister was an actress?" Amy queried thoughtfully.

"Yes." Colleen was uncomfortable, acutely aware that Amy was already hoping for far too much. Damn it, she didn't want her sister to be disappointed. And though she could hardly shield her from everything, she could cushion whatever blows came by trying to bring Amy back down to earth.

"And?" Amy prompted agitatedly, pacing back and forth.

"And nothing," Colleen said regretfully. "He mentioned vaguely he'd like to meet you sometime, but that was all."

She'd expected a tearful reproach from her sister for not having pinned him down about a time and place. Instead Amy gave a jubilant shout. "Oh, Colleen, I knew you'd do it for me!"

"Amy, calm down. It's not as if I arranged for an audition." Tempering Amy's expectations was turning out to be harder than she'd thought.

"But you helped me just the same, by letting him know I exist." Amy paused, thoughtfully tapping her foot. Colleen's wary look did nothing to quell her sister's joy; she simply said, "Oh, stop looking at me as if I were leading us both to the guillotines. Don't you think I realize it's up to me to make my own opportunities?"

"What do you mean it's up to you to make your own opportunities?" Colleen followed her through the swinging kitchen door as Amy danced her way into the living room, picked up her script and waltzed around with it perched on top of her head. "Amy, you're not going to do anything crazy, are you?" She knew from her years in New York the quest for a role could be an exercise in resourcefulness, to say the least. And the older the actors and actresses got, the more inventive they often became. Amy thought like someone who had been in the trade for fifteen or twenty years.

"Crazy, no. Attention getting, yes. What do you think about a telegram? Any chance he'd even see one from me, much less read it? Maybe I could send him a picture. Or copies of those reviews I got for my role as Helen Keller in *The Miracle Worker* last year. Maybe I could pretend to be a singing telegram from one of his friends!"

"Hold it right there," Colleen warned. "You are not sending anything to Lyon at his hotel. Just telling you where he was staying and in what room was a breach of ethics on my part. And it would be an unconscionable invasion of his privacy. Honey, we could both be sued if you were to bother him there. So please, don't do anything rash. Maybe—maybe we could get you an agent."

Amy brightened momentarily, then turned glum again. "Even if we did, it wouldn't help me in time for this movie." And they both knew how few movies were filmed in Columbus. "I guess you're right; it wouldn't be fair to bother him at his hotel." Swallowing hard, Amy gathered up her script and started for the stairs, saying, "I'd better be getting to bed. I've got my ACT college entrance exam tomorrow morning and play practice in the afternoon."

Colleen hated herself for having had to crush Amy's hopes, but she didn't want her to be hurt by building on unrealistic expectations. "I'll see you tomorrow then," she said softly.

"Good night." Amy's expression was despondent.

Colleen switched off all the lights and locked the door, then went upstairs. She washed her face, changed into her nightgown and turned out her bedside lamp, then lay in the dark wondering how to make her sister happy and still ensure that her future security wasn't in jeopardy. And then there was the matter of her own infatuation with Lyon. Just as she was drifting into a restless sleep, the telephone rang, jarring her awake. She fumbled for the lamp, then pulled the phone into bed with her and croaked, "Hello?"

"Miss Chandler?" The male voice on the other end of the line was genial but abrupt. "This is Harcourt Toland from the city desk of the Columbus Sunrise News." She recalled the journalist's name from her father's days as a senator. She remembered him as being a nice man who was nonetheless tenacious when it came to his work. "I'm calling to confirm a story one of our reporters has turned in."

"I'm sorry. I don't..." Bewilderment colored the tone of her voice as she struggled to make sense of what he was saying. "What story?"

A sleepy Amy stood silhouetted in the doorway. Colleen signaled her with a wave that everything was under control, not really sure that it was.

"We have a photo here of you with director Lyon Haggerty. It was taken at the Arlington Heights' football game this evening. Would you care to comment on how you know Mr. Haggerty or what your relationship to him is?"

Colleen's hand tightened on the receiver as she groaned inwardly. If she explained that she had cut Lyon's hair and then gone out with him on the spur of the moment, it would not look good for her. A report that Colleen had picked up a customer would hurt her business, perhaps irreparably. And she depended upon her income from the Trendsetter Salon to support herself and Amy. Her reply was reflective and as calm as she could make it. "No, I don't have any comment to make."

There was a rustle of paper on the other end of the line, and when he spoke again Harcourt's voice was weary. Apparently he didn't like verifying an item like this any more than she liked answering his questions. "A second report says you two dined at Spinelli's Pizza Parlor. Would you confirm that? Or where you and Mr. Haggerty went later?"

She didn't see that it was any of the city's business. Nevertheless she knew details of her date would probably appear in the morning paper. "No comment," she repeated firmly.

"Thank you anyway, Ms Chandler. I'm sorry to have bothered you." The phone clicked as he hung up.

Colleen broke the connection and dropped the receiver onto the floor, then smothered it with a pillow. Story or no story, she wanted to sleep for the rest of the night.

"Who was that?" Amy moved into the room.

"A reporter." She smothered a yawn. "He'd heard I was with Lyon and wanted the story confirmed."

"Why didn't you just admit it and let it go?"

"Because it wouldn't have stopped there. And because it's no one's business but mine who I see in my private life."

Amy seated herself on the edge of the bed. In the moonlight, resting her chin drowsily on her fist, she looked young and very vulnerable, and Colleen ached with a rush of protective feelings.

"How do you think Lyon's going to take it?"

"He's probably used to it," Colleen decided. But after Amy had gone back to her bed, she was left to wonder if that was true. Or maybe it would make a difference to him. Maybe in an effort to make his Ohio stay simpler and less locally newsworthy he'd decide not to see her any more. It wasn't a comforting thought.

Though the phone was off the hook for the duration of the night, Colleen didn't get much sleep. Finally, shortly after dawn, she showered and dressed and picked up the latest edition of the Columbus Sunrise News from the doormat. As much as she hated to look, she had to discover what had been printed. The item about Lyon Haggerty dating her headlined the Personalities column.

Spectators at the Arlington High game were stunned to recognize a celebrity in their midst. Lyon Haggerty, renowned film director, is here in town to complete work on his latest film—a teenage comedy that has reportedly already been cast. He was accompanied by the beautiful, elusive Colleen Chandler, proprietress of the Trendsetter Salon and daughter of the late United States Senator Aaron Chandler. Mr. Haggerty was unavailable for comment before press time. When reached late last night, Ms Chandler declined to make a comment.

Accompanying the article was a photo of Lyon standing in the crowd, signing autographs. Colleen was a step above him on the bleachers, her hands loosely encircling his elbow. She'd been attempting to convey to him the fact she wasn't running off, but merely making her way to the gates to meet him later, after the crowds had dispersed. However it looked as if she were holding on for dear life. Colleen groaned. It was a wonder, all things considered, they hadn't captioned the photo "Senator's Daughter Reels in Big Hollywood Fish." Heaven knows what a tabloid would have made of the photo.

Lyon was at her front door by eight o'clock. Colleen drew him inside and, glancing at the Saturday morning paper in his hand, felt a pang of sympathy for the man. "Sorry about the article."

"I'm used to it. I guess, having grown up in the limelight, you must be, too." Despite the early hour he looked wonderful; bright-eyed and fresh as if he'd just stepped out of the shower. Colleen inhaled the tangy scent of his after-shave with pleasure.

Lyon, in turn, seemed entranced by the curve of her thighs beneath the cream-colored gabardine slacks. A wave of shyness overwhelmed her and suddenly aware of the possibility of reporters, Colleen asked, "Did anyone see you come in?" She wished the coral turtleneck sweater she wore wasn't quite so soft or clinging and that his gaze was less intense.

"Do the three neighbors who rushed out in bathrobes to get a look at me and converse about the weather before asking for autographs count?"

She looked him up and down trying to judge his sincerity. "You're kidding."

"Nope, I'm not." He shrugged out of his light leather jacket and tossed it over the back of her sofa. "But I suppose you're more interested in the Nikon-wielding type who hide in trees than your neighbors, pleasantly nosy as they all are."

This was worse than she had ever imagined. "Did you see any reporters?" She didn't even want to think about what the neighbors might have asked.

He shook his head. "No. But you know the damned press and their telephoto lenses. And if any of the supermarket scandal sheets get hold of the fact we were together, no matter how innocently, you're liable to have ingenious paparazzi behind every shrub." His eyes were dark, direct and searching. He wanted her to know what she was in for if they continued to see each other. Calmly he related, "I found out this morning that Harcourt Toland had called my hotel for a confirmation. Because I had asked not to be disturbed, the front desk hadn't put his call through last night. I couldn't very well have denied we'd been together, and somehow 'no comment' always manages to look guiltier than the facts when in print."

She flushed, realizing that was exactly what she had said.

He shrugged. "Not that it would have mattered what I said to Toland. I found out he'd talked to you and several eyewitnesses from the game, confirming the bare facts to a printable degree. The same story and photo that ran in the Sunrise News had already been picked up by the wire services and printed in this morning's edition of the Maryland, Washington and L.A. papers."

Colleen groaned.

"My publicist called to give me the cheery news. She couldn't have been more delighted, though the film company was less than thrilled. They want me working twenty-four hours a day, with no time off for play." His tone softened as he added, "Apparently, because your dad was in politics, news of our liaison is of particular interest in D.C."

Just one date with Lyon and she already felt as if she were living under a microscope. "This is crazy."

"No, with me it's par for the course." His droll tone indicated he did not foresee it getting any better. When his eyes flicked briefly to her mouth, she wondered if he was thinking about the passionate kiss they had shared.

"So what now?" she asked breathlessly. Surely he hadn't come here just to convey bad news. Colleen dared to think that maybe he already cared about her as much as his searing gaze seemed to indicate.

"You tell me," he said softly. "How does this make you feel?" The ringing of the phone cut off whatever reply Colleen might have given. It was an old friend of the family, calling from Maryland to ask about the story. Blushing fiercely, she murmured yes, no, no, at intervals while Lyon roamed the room, appreciatively taking in the decorative touches—the bric-a-brac adorning the bookshelves and the art on the walls. She was glad he liked her home. Her friend's interrogation completed, Colleen placed the receiver back on the hook, then took it off to cover it with a pillow.

He looked askance at the muffled beeping bundle. "You do that often?"

"Since Toland phoned last night, I haven't felt much like taking calls." In fact she'd only put it back on the hook moments before he'd arrived.

"You could get an answering machine."

She could also toughen up, get used to such press scrutiny.

At the unexpected sound of a throat being cleared, they turned in tandem toward the carpeted spiral staircase. Seeing Amy, Colleen cringed and closed her eyes briefly, sensing that an impromptu audition was about to start while Lyon's eyes widened receptively.

Amy was clad in a white terry-cloth robe that swathed her from throat to toe. Before either of them could speak, Amy slipped effortlessly into character and began a letter-perfect rendition of a suburban mother agonizing over her lost child. The scene and wardrobe selection were both quite obviously from one of Lyon's early films.

Colleen, embarrassed beyond belief, started to move forward to interrupt, but Lyon's hand closed discreetly over her wrist, applying pressure until Colleen was mutely acquiescent beside him. The message from Lyon was to let her sister finish. Glancing at his face, Colleen saw he was spellbound by Amy's charisma and astonishingly riveted by the unscheduled audition.

Finished that monologue, Amy removed her robe to reveal tan corduroy pants, shirt and sweater. She slapped a jaunty-looking fedora on her head and assumed the role of a World War II adventuress looking for treasure. Lyon was silent, in awe, as Amy completed her enactment of the second scene, so different in mood and execution from the first, yet flawlessly played. There had been something different and something of Amy in each part. Charisma, personality, whatever that special quality was that made an actor or actress a screen presence, Amy had it.

Removing her hat, long hair flowing beautifully over her shoulders to her waist, Amy came the rest of the way down the stairs.

"Lyon, my sister, Amy," Colleen said dryly.

"Pleased to meet you." Lyon held out his hand, amusement dancing in his eyes.

What could have been a disaster turned out to be a pleasant interlude. Lyon asked a few questions about Amy's experience in the local community theatre and offered her encouragement with a dazzling smile. Amy responded with both compliments and mild critiques of every movie he'd made, somehow managing to treat Lyon as casually as if he was a meter reader for the power company. When she stalked determinedly over to extract a résumé and manila folder of glossy photos from the bookshelf near the door, Colleen couldn't help but admire her nerve.

Grinning impishly, Amy confided, "Colleen made me swear I wouldn't storm your hotel. But this morning's opportunity to audition was really too good to miss. However, now that you've seen me—" she shrugged into her jacket and slung a bag over her shoulder "—I've really got to go. First dress rehearsal of our play at the community theatre is this afternoon and we still have some last-minute work to do on the sets. I also have my college boards this morning, and if I don't run, I really will be late." Looking a bit uncertain now that the initial meeting had been pulled off, she dashed across the room and out the door, closing it swiftly behind her.

Both amused and embarrassed, Colleen had no idea what to say.

"Gutsy young lady, isn't she?" Lyon laughed, saving her from having to speak first. He shot her a contemplative look. "I assume that run-through means she knows I'm looking for an actress?"

"No," Colleen admitted. "Believe it or not, she doesn't. I couldn't think of a way to tell her, without having her overreact. She was so excited just to hear you were in town...."

"She has a certain presence." Lyon rubbed at his freshly shaved jaw. "Maybe I should hire her as an extra." He turned back to Colleen, his gaze direct. "Would I have your permission to give Amy a screen test, providing of course she's interested in appearing in my film? I'm not making any promises, you understand."

Colleen nodded. "As long as it doesn't interfere with her schoolwork or her appearance in the community play."

He smiled agreeably. "I think something could be arranged."

Abruptly Colleen realized she wasn't being a very gracious hostess. "Look, would you like some coffee?" she offered cordially. "I just finished brewing a pot."

"Please." Aware of his gaze upon her, she led him into the kitchen and poured coffee into two mugs. They sat at the kitchen counter, Lyon hooking the heels of his boots over the rungs of his stool. She sensed he had something important he wanted to discuss.

"I shouldn't hold you up this morning," he began. "I assume you have to work today?"

She nodded, her breath halting momentarily at his serious tone. Saturday was their busiest day in the salon.

Lyon continued gently, "I just wanted to discuss how to handle future inquiries into our relationship. Maybe nothing more will come of it, but we ought to be prepared. You must realize that, like it or not, anyone I date is of interest to the press. Your father having been a senator just adds a little more glitz to what would already be a hot new story for the gossip columns. Which is why, when asked by Harcourt Toland precisely what our relationship was, I purposely downplayed our date. I told him that, upon the referral of a hotel employee, I'd commissioned you to cut my hair. We struck up an immediate rapport, and as a personal favor you offered to show me a bit of local color while I was in town. We went to the game, had a late bite to eat. End of story."

He made it sound so inconsequential her heart sank. She might have guessed someone as celebrated as Lyon would handle the situation with more aplomb than she. "Thanks." The word was wrenched from her mouth. She felt as if her smile was frozen on her face. She got up to roam the kitchen.

He followed, his voice low when he spoke. "But that didn't cover half of what I felt."

His palms rested lightly on her shoulders, stirring up instant memories of his touch and kiss. "Have dinner with me tonight," he urged softly, planting a light kiss on her brow.

She swayed against him unsteadily, wanting to say no, but unable to. She had already decided by continuing to see Lyon she was bound to get hurt.

As if sensing her thoughts, he hooked his arm around her waist and pulled her toward him until they were touching in one long electrified line from her breasts to his thighs. "We could go somewhere quiet, somewhere out of town, anywhere you'd like," he coaxed in a warm erotic whisper that sent shivers up and down her spine.

His hands pressed against her spine, urging her closer, sliding upward ever so slowly to lightly trace her neck. Her nerve endings came to life under his gentle ministrations. Threading his fingers through her hair, he tilted her face up to his. Stillness pooled between them, their breaths meshing warmly, his mouth lowered and softly took hers. Erotic sensations blazed across her lips, and they parted in surrender to the warm pressure of his tongue. Her full breasts molded against the muscled contours of his chest, the thin lacy bra beneath her sweater no protection at all from the voluptuous sensations of pressure and heat. Her arms wreathed his neck and her fingers instinctively slid through the wheat-gold hair at his neck. He sighed, deep and low in his chest, kissing her with a hunger as deep and relentless and unquenchable as her own. Acutely aware of the warm unrelenting proof of the desire pressing against her, she moaned and clung to him. She felt as if she had been waiting her entire life for this moment, this man. A hunger was building deep inside her and wantonly she thrust against him, his hand pressing into the small of her back as she arched and moved seductively against him.

But then Lyon drew back, his breathing ragged, and valiantly reasserted his self-control. "If I thought you wouldn't regret this later..." His eyes told her of all the passion and sensual delights he wanted to share with her.

Colleen was brought back rudely to her senses, and placing her forearms and palms flat against the steely plane of his chest, she wedged some distance between them. His eyes darkened in resignation but never left her face.

"I wish I were different," she said finally.

He shook his head. "No you don't. And neither do I."

Beneath her splayed fingers she could feel the rapid drumming of his heart, the tense rigidity of every superbly formed muscle. Bewitching emotions shot through her as she again felt the evidence of his desire. Drawing her to him, he embraced her wordlessly, possessively, and kissed her gently. The need to be with him burned on inside her, raging out of control, and she knew it would go on burning, even after he was gone.

THE TRENDSETTER was buzzing with activity when Colleen walked through the gleaming glass-and-stainless-steel doors.

"Well, if it isn't the most sought-after young woman in all of the Buckeye state," Blake Hoskins announced dryly, holding up the society page of the morning paper. The most successful of her male stylists, the six foot four, 220-pound man was a former tackle for the Cleveland Browns. A leg injury had ended his football career at the age of twenty-seven. At first he had modeled for the Trendsetter's ads, but a love of women, a good eye and marvelously adept hands had led him to obtain his license as a stylist. He had become one of Colleen's best friends, and aside from Amy, he was her sole confidant.

"I can't believe you really went out with anyone that fabulous!" gushed punk-rock-loving Pansy Sims. "You've got to tell me what he's really like!"

"What who's like?" Colleen took off her coat and hung her bag in the locker. Feigning innocence, she stopped in front of a mirror to comb her fingers through her gleaming hair.

"Come on, Colleen," Blake demanded jokingly, ushering his client into the chair, which he then pumped up to a suitable height using his foot. "Confess the whole story before Pansy dies of curiosity."

"What's to confess?" Colleen held up her palms. "I cut the man's hair. Later he asked me out. I went."

Blake's eyes glimmered as if he saw right through her nonchalance, but he said nothing in response.

"And that's it?" Nineteen-year-old Pansy was crushed.

Colleen nodded, finding to her surprise that when under fire she was just as adept as Lyon at adapting a blasé tone. "He wanted to see some local color, so I took him to a football game."

Pansy was incredulous. "Couldn't you have taken him to one of the more popular clubs down by the Ohio State campus?" Dressed in tight leather pants and a form-fitting T-shirt, she was clearly the most unorthodox member of the staff.

Colleen paused to check the appointment book, then admitted wryly, "We were hoping we wouldn't be recognized. Unfortunately, Lyon was, so we had to cut the evening short." Colleen greeted her first client of the day, a sales representative for a local data-processing firm. After shampooing the young man's hair she led him back to her station, where group conversation resumed.

"Gee, I wonder why Lyon Haggerty picked you." Pansy mused thoughtfully, waving her comb and scissors in the air. "According to *Star Time* magazine he usually just dates starlets or—"

"Pansy," Blake tactfully interrupted, averting what she was about to say. "There are better periodicals you could be reading."

"I know," Pansy shot back. "*Sports Illustrated* for one. Don't think I didn't see you studying that bathing-suit issue!"

Blake shrugged. "Can I help it if I love beautiful women?"

Pansy snipped away at the split ends on the shocking but stylish Mohawk hairstyle her client had chosen. "Make fun of me if you want, Blake, but more often than not, *Star Time* is accurate—at least where the Hollywood scene is concerned. And they've printed a lot about Lyon, too. For instance, this new movie he's about to start filming is supposed to make every one of the newcomers he has chosen a major star."

"They always say that," Colleen murmured as she trimmed her client's sideburns, adjusting them to the middle of his ear. But her thoughts drifted to her sister. It would be wonderful for Amy if she did get a part, even a very small one.

The woman Blake was working on swiveled around toward Colleen. She seemed impressed that Colleen had actually dated the elusive filmmaker. "There was an article about Lyon Haggerty in last month's issue of *Celebrities*. Now that's a reputable magazine. Did you see it?"

Pansy snapped her fingers. "That's right! Lyon was in the September issue of *Celebrities*!" She put down her comb, and after apologizing to her client for the interruption, rushed over to the waiting area, where several stacks of magazines sat on low tables. "I know the very article you're talking about!" she exclaimed as she rifled the journals excitedly. "It's here somewhere...."

Blake grinned, then turned to Colleen. "So tell us more, boss. Does the man have any faults?" He seemed to sense how enamored Colleen was of the man, not a common occurrence by a long shot, for her.

Lyon had no faults Colleen could see, but for the amusement of the three clients, who were all ears, she said tongue-in-cheek, "I don't know any fan mag info—like what kind of sheets he sleeps in, how often they're changed, what he wears to bed or what he eats for breakfast. To be perfectly honest, he looks like a Wheaties man to me. I can tell you he likes pizza with everything but anchovies and doesn't care much when or how his hair is cut as long as it doesn't get into his eyes when he's trying to work."

"Didn't you ply him with alcohol and get any juicy gossip out of him?" Blake's tone was teasing.

"Sorry. He didn't drink anything stronger than hot chocolate or root beer."

Her interrogator groaned. "You'll never make the scandal sheets with dull fare like that."

It was Colleen's turn to grin complacently. "I know."

Pansy came back waving a magazine with Lyon's picture on the cover. Dressed in jeans and a faded blue chambray shirt worn open to the waist, he was relaxing on the dunes at Big Sur. The photo, fetching as it was, couldn't begin to capture the man's magnetism, but Colleen eyed the article greedily. Anxious as she was to read it, she carefully cut and styled the salesman's hair and treated her next client, a matronly buyer for a large department store, with extra care. Luckily, her third client of the morning was slightly late; she was dying of inquisitiveness. As nonchalantly as possible, she picked up the magazine and headed back toward the Coke machine.

"I knew she couldn't last for long!" she heard Blake crow after her. "If curiosity killed, Colleen would be the first to go."

"Ho, ho." Colleen remarked, face flaming. With relief, she shut the lounge door and settled down with a cold diet drink to read. Unfortunately, the article only strengthened her misgivings about Lyon.

Entitled "I'll Never Marry Again," the story centered on Lyon's reportedly very painful divorce some two-and-a-half years earlier and his adjustment since.

He had acquired, along with his film successes, the trappings of a confirmed bachelor. He owned a beachhouse in Malibu, an estate in Bel Air, a penthouse in New York and a chalet in Vail, Colorado. He'd built his parents a lavish new home, put two of his brothers and one of his sisters through college. He worked for and contributed lavishly to the Special Olympics and did sixty-second commercials for the United Way, making use of his generous talents both in front of the camera as a spokesperson for important causes, and behind it, as a director. When asked what he looked for in female companions, he was quoted as saying, "I'll tell you this. I don't much care if she can cook or clean house."

Colleen winced as she recalled when asked about her hobbies by Lyon, she'd admitted to gourmet cooking and parenting her baby sister. Domestic activities both.

Accompanying the article were pictures of Lyon with a succession of lady loves, many of them actresses who had starred in his films. Featured most prominently was a television-turned-film actress named Roxanne Stuart. Blond, beautiful and very well endowed, she had made waves with a wet-T-shirt poster several years before. There was Lyon, in black tie at last year's Academy Awards, with Roxanne on his arm, and Lyon, relaxing at his Malibu beach hideaway with another beautiful bikini-clad companion, identified only as "Roxanne's successor," stretched voluptuously out beside him. The last photo was of Lyon, alone on the deck of his Vail retreat, watching the sun go down behind the tree-covered mountain slopes.

"Colleen, next client's here!" Pansy stuck her head in the lounge door.

The phone rang continually all morning; Colleen's friends and acquaintances, some of whom she hadn't heard from for years, seemed to be crawling out of the woodwork. Colleen took the first two calls, repeated her embarrassed repertoire of one yes and half a dozen no's, then gave it up and told the Trendsetter receptionist to take messages or to tell callers that she'd be unavailable for the next three weeks—for as long as Lyon was in town—but would write when she could.

Two o'clock brought an AP stringer into the shop, wanting a hot scoop, which she declined to give him. When he persisted Blake ushered him out. An offer from someone who claimed to represent the tabloid *Star Time* came by phone an hour later. They, too, wanted her to tell all. She tore up the message.

"I think I'm beginning to know what it must feel like to get hit by a Mack truck," she said wearily.

"Awesome," Pansy mused. "You really could be famous."

Unfortunately, famous was not what Colleen wanted to be.

Amy met Colleen at the door when she got home at five-thirty. Seeing her sister's glowing expression, Colleen commented, "You must have aced your entrance exams."

For a split second the glow on the younger woman's face faded. "Not exactly." Amy shifted indecisively. "I didn't take them." Taking a deep breath, she rushed on before Colleen could comment. "I went to audition for Lyon Haggerty instead. I did it, Colleen! I actually got the part! I, Amy Chandler, am going to play the mayor's daughter in Lyon's new film!"

She clasped her hands together and closed her eyes, savoring the memory. "Oh, Colleen, you should have been there. It was like something out of a movie magazine. I was actually on camera. They did a screen test on the spot, developed the film, viewed it, everything!"

"Slow down." Numb, Colleen sank into a nearby chair. "You're sure you've got the part?" She wondered if Amy had somehow misunderstood what had been decided.

"Positive! Lyon's going to discuss the terms of my employment with you over dinner this evening. Or he said he could get me an agent to negotiate the deal on my behalf. Or we could see a lawyer. But I don't care about that!"

Colleen cared; she didn't want Amy signing her life away. And she didn't even know what the movie was about.

Amy rushed over to sit cross-legged in front of Colleen. "Just think, after we're done here with the location scenes I'll get to move to Los Angeles. Oh, Colleen, isn't it just too much!"

It certainly was. "What do you mean you get to move to Los Angeles? Who said anything about moving?" What had Lyon gotten them into? Damn it, if he hurt Amy, even inadvertently, she'd kill him!

Amy was too overjoyed to pick up on her sister's heartfelt reservations. "Lyon says it'll take two or three months of filming in L.A. to finish the movie." She continued on a calmer note. "Then I could come back, though by that time I imagine I'll want to stay on, particularly if I'm offered another job."

Dread settled over Colleen. Why hadn't Lyon discussed this with her this morning? When he'd mentioned testing Amy for a small part, she'd assumed he'd been talking only about scenes that would be shot there in Columbus. Never had he said anything about Amy having to go to Los Angeles!

Both hands clasped under her chin, Amy leaned forward imploringly. "You don't look very happy. Don't you understand what this means to me? My film career has been launched!"

Her sister's naïveté made Colleen wince. She was talented, yes, but very inexperienced when it came to matters of the real world. It would be so easy for anyone in the film community to take advantage of her. Gently she tried to put things back into their proper perspective. "What about your play at the community theatre?"

"Oh, I'm out of that," Amy said confidently.

Colleen was at a complete loss. Everything was happening too fast—and she had been asked to confer on precious little of it!

"You're mad at me for skipping my college entrance exam, aren't you?" Amy returned reluctantly.

"You needed those test scores in order to apply for a scholarship." In a moment of ambitious impulsiveness Amy had practically thrown everything away and she didn't even seem aware of it.

"I'll take them when they're offered next spring." She waved away Colleen's concern.

Colleen stared at Amy in shocked silence. Where was the responsible young woman she had helped raise? "The scholarships will all be given out by then, Amy. It will be too late to qualify for anything other than a student loan. More importantly, the prestigious drama schools may already have filled their classes."

Amy lifted her shoulders in a careless shrug. "So I won't go to college."

Colleen shook her head, defeated. Dreams of instant success were nice, being disillusioned and disheartened at an early stage in life wasn't. And Amy had already had more than her share of heartbreak and hard times in her young life. "Going to college was part of our deal," she cautioned.

Amy got up to pace the room, shoving her hands down into the pockets of her pants. "We made that pact about me going to school before Lyon came to town."

Colleen could see she was to have a royal battle on her hands. Still, she tried to maintain her composure, saying reasonably, "Amy, you need your education."

"Not as much as I need this part." Her chin was set stubbornly. "Lyon said you wouldn't be happy about this."

"You discussed me?" Colleen stared at her sister in stupefaction. He had betrayed her!

Amy nodded. "But I was so dumb, I wouldn't listen to him. He asked me to wait and let him break the news to you himself during your date. Like a fool, I told him it wasn't necessary. I thought...I thought you'd be happy for me!"

But Lyon had known differently. Damn him! He must know Amy wasn't ready to handle the ups and downs of Hollywood! She could feel her temper soaring out of control. The brunt of her anger was no longer directed at Amy but at Lyon. Amy had her youth and her innocence as an excuse. Lyon had neither.

"You don't want me working for him, do you?" Amy accused resentfully.

"I think there is a lot you haven't stopped to think about," Colleen answered pragmatically, thinking of everything that could go wrong. Having had entry into the world of show business through many of her clients in New York, Colleen knew that an actress could be replaced as easily as she could be hired. What then, she wondered. It might ruin Amy's reputation, alter her entire future. The more she thought about it, the more furious she became with Lyon for not having at least consulted her. But those were fears she couldn't, wouldn't voice to Amy.

"Lyon will see that my interests are taken care of," Amy retorted defiantly, tenaciously clinging to her dream.

In Colleen's opinion, he hadn't done a very good job of that so far. But it was obvious that Amy had steeled herself against any arguments, no matter how reasonable.

"What could possibly happen, Colleen? This is my big chance!"

Maybe so, maybe not. Either way, if Amy had gotten herself into something unpalatable, Colleen was going to be forced to play the heavy in order to get her out of it. It was a nasty position to be in, one

that was potentially damaging to her relationship
with Amy, and she blamed Lyon. If he had just come
to her first for permission.... Damn him anyway!

Colleen was so furious, she didn't trust herself to
speak! And she was certainly in no shape to counsel
her sister. "Look, I've got to go out." She stood up
and reached for her coat, determined to find Lyon
and tell him what she thought of his underhanded
actions.

"Colleen, you're not going to ruin things for me!"
Amy caught her arm imploringly.

Colleen paused at the door. "I've got to check into
this."

"You can't talk to Lyon if you're mad at him!" Amy
wailed, near tears. "If he gets mad at you, it might
ruin everything for me!"

"Honey, I have to go. You did say earlier that Lyon
thought I might be angry, so he'll probably be prepared for it. It's my responsibility as your guardian
to see that your interests really are protected."
Heaven knew, their parents wouldn't have ap-
proved of the recent turn of events, a fact that made
Colleen feel all the more guilty. She had failed them
all miserably by not paying more attention to what
Amy had clearly been contemplating from the moment she heard Lyon was in town. The signs had
been there; Colleen simply hadn't reacted respon-
sibly, mainly because she herself had been so infa-
tuated with Lyon.

Amy warned heatedly, "Colleen, if you ruin this for me, I'll never speak to you again." It was precisely that kind of threat Colleen had hoped to avoid. "And besides, I'm going to be eighteen in another month. You can stop me now, but..."

A heavy silence fell over the room. Amy turned away, her shoulders shaking with emotion and as yet unshed tears.

"I'll be back in a while," Colleen said quietly, and walked through the door. If Lyon had caused a rift between her and Amy, Colleen would never forgive him.

5

"HOW COULD YOU have offered Amy the part without at least consulting me?" Colleen was demanding furiously a scant half an hour later.

All too aware of the film people milling about the penthouse suite of the Regency, Lyon backed her out into the hallway, closing the door behind him. Her heels dug into the plush carpet defensively at the intensity of his look and she was reminded that she had just barged in uninvited, not even pausing at the front desk to let someone announce her presence.

Lyon's incisive gaze traveled over Colleen. His jaw tensed, but his voice was calmly emphatic when he spoke. "I did ask your permission to test her for the part."

"A small part as an extra. You didn't say anything about her moving to Los Angeles." She felt grimy and tired after a day at the salon and now this. Never had she felt so betrayed.

A sigh of exasperation hissed through his teeth. "This isn't the time to discuss it, Colleen."

"I'm not leaving until we do."

He grabbed her hand then and held it in a vicelike grip. Turning back toward his suite, he opened the door, and with a roguish smile, he called to his fellow workers, "We'll have to continue this later, folks. Something important has come up."

There was a murmur of teasing response, and many curious glances Colleen's way. But the group departed obediently.

After he shut the door Lyon focused once again on Colleen. In the absence of others, the room seemed unnaturally silent. Lyon's smile faded. She could hear the rhythm of her own breathing and see the controlled rising and falling of his chest. He, too, looked like he had suffered a very tiring, trying day but she refused to feel the least bit of sympathy for him. Instead she extricated herself from his grip with a defiant yank of her hand.

He made no effort to recapture his hold on her. His eyes swept over her and then returned to her face. She recalled the last time they had met, their steamy embrace, and got the impression that it was all he could do not to drag her into his arms. Keeping his distance, he said only, "Look, I don't know what Amy told you. . ." He waved a hand toward the couch.

Colleen remained where she was, ignoring his invitation to sit and discuss things more civilly. She wanted to hold tight to her anger. It was a source of power and strength. Her spine was ramrod straight.

"She told me enough for me to know she's in way over her head."

Lyon's mouth thinned at her disparaging assessment. "You're saying I took advantage of her?" He threw the pen he had been carrying onto the table.

"Didn't you?"

He stared at her incredulously. "No, I did not." The words were terse.

She drew in a sharp breath, furious. "Are you aware that Amy skipped her college entrance exam this morning?"

"Yes." Ignoring her refusal to sit, he braced a hip on the back of the sofa, the casual action belying the angry light in his eyes.

"But you let her read for you anyway."

He lifted both hands in a conciliatory gesture that irritated her immensely. The edges of his mouth curled upward in a mocking smile. "What would you have had me do when she showed up at the auditions? Throw her out on the street? I thought she deserved the chance to read." His voice held the steel of conviction. "As it turned out, she was perfect for the role. I'm sorry you found out about it the way you did. I wanted to tell you myself."

She had expected him to be more apologetic, more soothing, not smouldering with his own fury. Heart thudding uncontrollably, she felt herself become even more defensive. Damn it, he was twisting this around and making her seem the villain! "Why? So you could sweet-talk me into allowing her to move to Los Angeles? Your telling me personally wouldn't have changed anything. Amy cannot take that part."

He stood slowly, his hands clenched at his sides, his mouth set. "You're making a mistake."

She shook her head. "No, you made a mistake when you put the needs of your film above the welfare of my sister."

He seemed to be having more trouble controlling his temper than she; a muscle worked convulsively in his cheek. "You don't have any idea how much this means to Amy, do you?"

The softly spoken words struck a chord, but she wouldn't let him sidetrack her with guilt. "Unfortunately, I do know. But that doesn't change what I think will be best for Amy in the long run."

"It changes everything!" At her sharp glance, he lowered his voice. "Look, success as an actor is based twenty-five percent on talent, twenty-five percent on luck and fifty percent on desire. Amy has that desire in abundance. In my estimation she'll never be happy unless she's allowed to act."

"No matter what it does to her to be thrust into the limelight at this vulnerable stage of her life?" Colleen was on the verge of exploding with anger.

Her accusation only made him calmer. "You've done a good job bringing her up; she's obviously got her head on straight. We spent a great deal of time interviewing her, as we did with all the kids involved in the project. If we didn't believe Amy could handle the demands and the pressure, she wouldn't have been given the part."

"You think I should just let her go, and to the devil with her education, with college," she spat.

"As Amy pointed out, in another month she will be eighteen years old. Then it won't matter what any of us says or advises, legally she'll be able to make her own decisions."

About that he was right. But it didn't mean that Amy had made the right choice today. Silence fell between them. She met his gaze in a defiant collision of wills.

He seemed to sense he was getting nowhere with her. "For pity's sake, Colleen, be reasonable!" he said roughly. "An appearance in my film is enough to get her noticed by every director and producer in the world!"

"And what then? What if no offers are immediately forthcoming? Her education will have been interrupted. She'll have no scholarship, no way of even going back to the local community theatre! I have a business here, Lyon, a business I can't possibly leave unattended for that length of time. I can't just pick up and move to Los Angeles for two or three months on a whim. Nor can I let Amy go to Los Angeles for that length of time alone."

"Now who's putting their own welfare first?"

Her face burned.

Apparently he regretted his words, and his voice became gentle. "If it's only her stay in Los Angeles you're worried about, something can be arranged. My assistant director, Samantha McCreary, has raised three teenagers. I'm sure she'd be glad to oversee Amy's care."

"Regardless of who chaperones Amy, I don't think this is the right move for her now. I'm not sure she can handle the emotional ups and downs of a film career."

Lyon strode to the window. Momentarily he was silent, taking in the scene before him. "I can understand your fears on that score, Colleen. But she'll have to learn to take it eventually. Maybe now is the best time."

"I don't agree." What Lyon was thinking she couldn't tell. But abruptly his attitude changed, his voice became reasonable. It was a guise Colleen distrusted even more. "Look, why don't you stay and have dinner..." he began softly, turning toward her.

Colleen stiffened. He seemed to think that given enough time, romantic opportunity and atmosphere, he could convince her of anything.

"No thanks." She started for the door.

He overtook her and stopped her easily, an arm across the doorframe, deliberately barring her way. Still watching her steadily, he stated precisely, "I want Amy in my picture."

"You want! What about what's best for Amy?"

He said nothing. And suddenly it seemed imperative she attack his motives as virulently as he had attacked hers. "You wouldn't let anything get in the way of turning out a successful picture, would you? Even my sister's future. What will this buy you, Lyon? Another mansion you can't possibly need?"

His features hardened. "As far as you're concerned, the verdict on me is already in, isn't it?" His voice held a note of contempt.

"You're damn right about that much!"

Pain flared briefly in his eyes. He moved aside to let her pass through the doorway. "Do what you want, Colleen. Amy can't legally act without your permission. Not yet. But bear in mind if you do refuse her this opportunity, you'll only make her more determined to go the Hollywood route. And in the process you'll probably have irreparably damaged your relationship with her." He paused. "On the other hand, were you to support her first film endeavor wholeheartedly, you'd be able to see her interests are well-protected contractually. I'll give you twenty-four hours to consent. After that I'll have no choice but to give someone else the role."

"You really want her in your picture that badly?" Tears of frustration burned her eyes.

"Enough to put up with your harassment."

Abruptly Colleen brushed past him into the hall and entered the waiting elevator. The doors closed swiftly and silently between them.

"SO WHAT HAPPENED?" Amy met her at the door. Colleen could tell she'd been crying, and her heart ached. She would have given anything to reverse this situation.

"We talked.... Lyon still wants you for the role. He's given us twenty-four hours to make a decision."

Colleen was weary, emotionally drained. On the ride home she had come to the realization that what Lyon had asserted was true. Amy was determined to do this, and only by capitulating could Colleen protect her sister's interests. She couldn't deny Amy, not now, not without causing a permanent breach in their relationship. She wondered bitterly if Lyon had been counting on that or if he had just not stopped to think about all the ramifications, so intent had he been on solving the casting problems of his movie.

"And?"

"Tell me more about the role," Colleen said quietly. If life as an actress was even one-tenth as hard as she had heard, Amy was going to need all the support she could get. "When does filming start?"

"Monday morning. The cast will be working here for three weeks. Then it's back to L.A. for another week of rehearsals and an additional two months of filming." Amy spoke hesitantly, as if afraid Colleen would still refuse to grant her permission to take the role.

"What about the hours?"

"By law all the kids who are under age must study three hours a day and work no more than four. Lyon told me they have a school on the set in L.A., and they'll be setting up a classroom here at the Regency, too. They prefer all the kids to stay at the hotel, so they can keep an eye on them and make sure they're available for rehearsal or costume fittings and tutoring sessions as need be. They have adult chaperons assigned to every suite. Their rules are very strict, Colleen; anyone caught breaking them is immediately fired."

Colleen realized belatedly Amy really had given a lot of thought to this. Perhaps more than she had.

"The movie is about growing up in the world today," Amy continued. "I have a script and I've already read it. It's a good film, Colleen, a really worthwhile project." She faced her sister hopefully. Clearly Amy had regained her perspective.

Reassured, Colleen began to relax. "I'm sorry I overreacted—"

Amy cut off her apology with a raised palm. "You were right to be upset with me. I shouldn't have skipped the entrance exam. And I should have asked your permission before I tried out. I'm sorry. But, Colleen, I was so afraid I'd lose the chance to audition or that if I didn't go right away Lyon would choose someone else. I knew what a long shot my getting the part was." She desperately wanted Colleen to understand.

Colleen did. But that didn't mean she would forgive Lyon.

6

"I DON'T THINK the entire problem is the perm. Your hair needs deep conditioning as well as a cut."

Colleen's client frowned deeply as she looked in the mirror. The twenty-eight-year-old homemaker and mother of two preschoolers had made a quantum leap from waist-length hair to a short and curly style, in an effort to make herself look more sophisticated. The result, unhappily, had been a disaster. Colleen could have cheerfully choked the unnamed stylist from another establishment who was responsible.

"I look so old."

Jan Barlow did look matronly. It had taken her three weeks to work up the nerve to come to Colleen, and though she'd made the appointment on the recommendation of a friend who regularly had her cut at the Trendsetter, Jan was obviously still nervous, her hands fidgeting beneath her cape. Colleen's heart went out to her. In some respects this was the type of client she enjoyed working with the most. "Do you trust me enough to let me cut your hair again?" she asked.

Jan bit her lip.

"We're not going to do it to please me, we're going to do it to please you," Colleen said softly, knowing how distressing it was to get an unattractive haircut.

"Okay." Jan's permission was given reluctantly. "I'm not used to short hair to begin with. And now this perm! I just can't do anything with it!"

"And you're afraid if we cut off more it will make it worse." Colleen read her mind sympathetically. Jan had a point. Her hair was in poor condition. Worse, it had a tendency to frizz. But those were flaws that could be corrected.

With an artistic eye, Colleen surveyed her client. "Let's take a minute and I'll show you what I intend to do. You do need a better cut, something that will fall into place with just a shake of your head. I can do that without sacrificing much of the length. You need fullness here on the sides but not too much fullness on top, or the result will be a disproportioned, dated look." As Colleen talked she demonstrated, by pulling up sections of hair to show Jan what she meant, where her hair was too long or too heavy. "I noticed you were wearing glasses when you came in. Do you wear them often?"

Jan nodded. "Nearly all the time. I tried contacts once, but they didn't work out."

"Okay. We'll want to take that into account and make sure that your bangs aren't too long or too heavy. When we get done, all you're going to have to do is wash, condition and finger-dry your hair. The result will be a soft swept-away look."

"Boy, you sure handled her well," Blake remarked after Jan had walked out an hour later, looking happy and carefree.

Colleen smiled. Nothing beat the feeling she had when a client left feeling better about herself. "You know how much difference the right hairstyle can make in the way a person looks and feels. It's more important than any makeup or clothing."

"Yeah," Blake said, "but I've never seen anyone who can size up a client faster or recognize precisely what is wrong with their hair."

She glowed in Blake's praise. "Practice makes perfect."

"No, in your case, talent and a genuine love of people make perfect. I think you ought to stick strictly to consultations and leave the regular work to us lackeys," he decided.

"Very funny. You know my regular clients would put up a howl that would be heard in Cleveland. As would yours," Colleen replied, sweeping the hair from the floor.

Blake shrugged. "I still think you're underestimating the depth of your talent."

"And you're underestimating yours." Blake had many of the same qualities. Living proof was the roster of socially prominent women who paid to have him cut and style their hair. With a few minutes between clients they adjourned to the lounge for a break.

"Have you seen much of Amy lately?" Blake asked, settling himself in a comfortable chair.

"Not since I helped her move into the hotel on Sunday afternoon. We've talked every night, though."

"How's she doing?"

"She's really happy with her work and excited. Says she's learning a lot." Without Amy their home seemed empty, her personal life even more desolate. Not even Colleen's absorption with her own work could ease the ache. "I've met the other kids in the film. They're all very nice, normal. Not the prima donnas I guess I half expected. They're well chaperoned, too. Samantha McCreary is in charge of the kids and she's particularly nice and levelheaded." About forty-five years old, Samantha was trim and relaxed, with a penchant for tennis shoes and jogging suits.

"Have you heard from Lyon?"

Blake alone had sensed how enamored Colleen had been of the man. But then the two of them had always been close, she reflected. She'd schooled Blake through the various breakups and reunions with his lady friends, and he had schooled her through her own dealings with the men in her life.

"No," she said evenly. "Samantha McCreary has handled everything since the audition; even the contracts were discussed with her." Colleen had taken them to her own attorney for approval. After some checking he had pronounced them more than fair. And the money Amy would be earning would enable her to go to college and pay her own way for several years if she so chose.

"You must feel reassured then," Blake observed.

"Yes," Colleen agreed. But no less angry with Lyon. Still, it was some consolation, knowing that Amy was happy.

THE REST OF HER WEEK passed slowly, without incident. Then came Friday morning, and the call from her sister.

"Colleen, you've got to help me!" Amy grabbed her sister's attention, her flair for high drama reflected in her urgent, slightly theatrical tone. "I'm in desperate trouble."

Alarm bells sounded in her head. "Calm down," Colleen advised, while panic rose in her. "And tell me what the problem is."

"I look terrible!" Amy wailed.

"Is that all?" Colleen relaxed.

"What do you mean is that all? This is my film debut!" Amy countered.

Immediately contrite, Colleen replied, "I'm sorry. I just... for a second I thought you'd been in an accident or something."

"She's right; we do have a problem," Lyon interjected tersely, unexpectedly taking over the phone. "We're doing this punk scene and nothing is working. The look is all wrong. Amy seems to think you can help." He seemed less sure. There was a lengthy pause. "Can you come over to the set?" He rattled off the name of the warehouse that was serving as the crew's base of operations.

"I could send Pansy—" Colleen offered. "She's our expert in punk looks."

"No, you can't. I've got a full schedule this afternoon," Pansy interrupted.

"Amy wants you," Lyon said firmly. "If nothing else you'll be able to give her some much needed moral support."

He sounded disgruntled and upset. Put that way, Colleen could hardly refuse. "What is it you want me to do?" Her tone was brisk and professional.

"Consult, offer suggestions," Lyon retorted in a clipped tone.

Amy got back on the phone. "Oh, please, Colleen, please!" Her voice was trembling. "You're the only one who can make me look really good punk!" she pleaded.

Colleen could tell that she was near tears, and she couldn't let her down. Blake agreed to take all her appointments for the rest of the day, after Colleen had swiftly rescheduled all those that could be moved for early the next week.

When she arrived they were setting up a scene in which the punk kids looked preppy and the preppy kids looked punk. And Lyon was right, Colleen observed, as soon as she arrived, nothing was working. Amy, in particular, was a mess. They had given her a short, half-carrot, half-scarlet-colored Mohawk wig. It was hideous.

Lyon came toward her. The tense set of his shoulders was the only clue to his distress. His voice was low, gravelly. "As the most prominent kid in the film, I wanted Amy to look spectacular and smashing."

"And less like a dog," Amy said glumly.

"Don't worry, honey, we'll fix it," Colleen reassured, then glanced at Lyon. She treated him with the respect and reserve she would have given a total stranger, nothing more, nothing less. "Is there a dressing room where we can work in private?"

He nodded and led them to one of the makeup trailers parked inside the warehouse. Quiet reigned when they shut the door behind them. Lyon lounged against the counter. Colleen would have preferred that Lyon not be present. But since he was the boss and had opted for a ringside seat, she had no choice. "Mind if we start from scratch?" She barely glanced his way.

"Be my guest."

While Amy used cold cream to cleanse the unflattering Pan-Cake from her face, Colleen assessed the problem. "Amy's main strength is her beautiful waist-length hair. It defines her. Therefore I think that you should keep it."

"You mean dye it?" Lyon asked, incredulously.

"Heavens, no!" Amy and Colleen both said in a horrified duet. Involuntarily, Amy had clutched her mane with the look of someone who would kill before she let herself be scalped, permed or bleached.

"But we do want to make her look the part. I suggest we have them send over a platinum-blond wig and then we can create an Indian-headdress look—the kind that the tribal chief would wear. Instead of feathers coming out from the face, though, it will be hair dyed a rainbow of colors, lifted and held in place with a heavy coating of styling gel. And since it will be a wig it won't have to be redone every time you shoot, either. We can use lavender eye shadow to bring out the blue in her eyes." Picking up a blank pad of paper and a pen, Colleen drew and illustrated as she talked. For a moment she forgot her anger at Lyon as her enthusiasm took over. "We'll use slashes of burgundy on her cheeks—it will have to be dramatic so maybe we can paint the blush on in sharp triangular wedges. Lip color should be different, something really bright for shock value. It will help make her really look punk. The mascara should be midnight blue, with thick black lines slashed emphatically above and below the eye."

Lyon looked pleased as he asked, "Can you do the makeup and hair? I'll double your normal out-of-salon fee."

"Sure."

Amy clasped her sister's hand and held on tight, making Colleen very glad she had come. Their business finished, Lyon let himself out of the trailer. When Amy's new look was finished, she was thrilled. "Far out," she said, assessing her new image in the mirror.

Lyon was called back into the trailer to check it out. After a moment he admitted admiringly, "I didn't think it was possible to be punk and pretty." His glance traveled over Amy and he frowned perplexedly. "But there's still something missing."

"It's the dress," Colleen said quietly, looking at the motorcycle-gang, black leather outfit Amy currently wore. The others around her concurred. "I would suggest something more feminine."

Lyon hesitated, unconvinced. "Such as?" His voice held a challenging tone.

Colleen shrugged. No one offered any suggestions, whether because Lyon had already exhausted the extent of their input or they wanted to see what Colleen could do, given the chance. She didn't know. Assured that she wasn't usurping anyone else's territory, she answered Lyon smoothly, "Anything that would give her a total put-together look." When Lyon still looked blank, she brainstormed.

"Maybe a short white leather Indian-style mini-dress dripping with fringe and sequins and beads, thigh-high boots, maybe either multicolored or fire-engine red."

The wardrobe lady agreed wholeheartedly, suggesting, "Add some black arm bands and gaudy jewelry, the black leather jacket, and you've got an ensemble."

Visualizing the suggested outfit, Lyon smiled. "You're right."

The wardrobe lady agreed to whip up a new outfit for Amy right away. Amy said goodbye to Colleen and ran over to participate in the blocking of the next scene to be filmed. Colleen looked at the clock realizing it was after six. Where had the time gone?

The trailer emptied out until only she and Lyon were left. "Thanks for coming today." Lyon's eyes met hers, curiously gentle. She resisted their magnetic appeal. She couldn't trust him, she thought, not when his first concern and his last was his movie.

"You're welcome." She busied herself stowing equipment into her carryall. Instead of rushing off to join the others, as she had half expected him to do, Lyon lingered, gallantly holding open the trailer door for her when she was ready to leave.

"If you'd like to stay on and observe..." he offered unexpectedly, after a moment.

The idea of watching Amy work was tempting. "No thanks. I've got to get back to the shop." Her tone was cool and impersonal. He gave her a searching look, as if trying to find a chink in her armor or at least a trace of the old anger. But she kept herself aloof. There was still a basic attraction between them, a primitive male-to-female pull. But she could and would fight it. Their romance was over. She wanted it to stay that way.

7

"AMY TOLD ME I might find you here." Lyon's voice startled Colleen, but she didn't turn to look at him.

With the weekend looming ahead like a yawning abyss, and Amy having to work, she had decided to drive out to the family farm, a much-used retreat for generations. Just being there always made her feel better.

"I needed to unwind." She'd been unusually tense after leaving the set yesterday. "It seemed a good time to come out and pick the last of the fall apples." The scent of ripe fruit filled the air. The wind was chill as it tossed strands of hair across her face and into her eyes. With one hand on the trunk of the tree for balance, her feet on the next to the top rung of a wooden ladder, Colleen tucked her hair behind her ear with her free hand.

"I need to ask a favor," he began reluctantly.

She resumed dropping apples in her bucket. He came around the base of the tree, glancing up at her. "Since you redid Amy's costume, I've been inundated with requests to have you do similar makeovers on the others."

She knew he would have much preferred her to come down the ladder and confront him at eye level. Perversely, she stayed where she was.

"Amy looks so much better than everyone else. It's only fair the others have the advantage of your artistic expertise, too. I'll pay you well."

Dusting off her hands, she rested the bucket on the apex of two spreading branches and, with one hand curved around a thick branch, pulled herself up to sit in the tree. "Wouldn't your other technicians resent that?"

They'd been cordial to her on Friday, true, but that may have been because she was Amy's sister, there only to help Amy.

"Frankly, the other stylists and makeup artists would welcome the chance to work with you again. Everyone was impressed with what you were able to do." He seemed finally to include himself in the tally.

Grudgingly she admitted, "I did enjoy working there."

"Then you'll help out?"

She nodded, still keeping a wary eye on him. "When do you need me?"

"Monday morning. Seven o'clock."

"I'll be there." She waited for him to leave, watching expressionlessly as he started to stride off; then he came back almost as an afterthought. A rueful expression crossed his face.

"Look, this is silly for us to be treating each other like strangers. Can't we be friends again?"

Dusk was descending in beautiful pinks and blues, mingling with gray streaks of sky. Colleen shifted restlessly on her perch, the bark rough beneath the fabric of her clothes, the palms of her hands. "I don't know. Can I trust you not to go behind my back with any more offers for my sister?"

He winced at her sarcastic tone. Then before she could stop him, he had mounted the ladder and worked his way up several steps until he was almost at eye level with her. Resting his elbow on the top of it, he explained reasonably in a soft tone that sent shivers down her spine, "That was more her doing than mine. She was waiting for me in the parking lot and followed me to auditions in her car. I didn't even see her!"

That, Colleen hadn't known. But it made sense. How else would Amy have known where to go? Lyon had never said where the auditions were being held. She refused to absolve him entirely of blame. "You didn't have to give her a chance to read." She wished she could find a way out of that tree. Staying up there after he had arrived had been a way of keeping herself invincible. Now, with him blocking the only easy way down, she felt trapped.

He leaned closer, resting his chin on his hand. She could smell the tang of his after-shave, see the sincerity in his eyes. "No, I didn't." He straightened resolutely. "But you know how much she wants to act. I would have been heartless to refuse her that chance. Besides that, she's good." He glanced at the fields around them. Overgrown with weeds, they had been fallow for years. A mixture of green and yellow leaves made a canopy over their heads.

She clung stubbornly to her anger. "The least you could have done was to ask my permission before you offered her the part." She met his glance with an accusing look.

His eyes darkened, but there was no other discernible change in his expression. "When Amy showed up at the audition, she led me to believe she had already discussed it with you by phone and obtained your permission. I didn't know until later, when you showed up at my hotel, that she hadn't. If I had known the depth of your reservations, I never would have given her the part, regardless of how right I thought she was for it. I'm not in the business of breaking up families."

"It seems I judged you unfairly." She studied him surreptitiously beneath lowered lashes. "Why didn't you tell me this before?"

"I probably should have, would have, if you hadn't been so furious to begin with."

"But then I made you angry, too." She admitted to herself that she'd done it deliberately, to wedge distance between them.

He studied her in silence for several moments. "This past week has been tough for you, hasn't it?"

After a moment she nodded. "It's been an emotionally trying time for me. I've worked so hard to give Amy a stable upbringing and I never figured on this happening."

"It's hard for you, letting her go."

Colleen nodded, tears blurring her eyes. As necessary a move as it was, it still hurt—a lot more than she had expected. "Not until she started working for you this past week did I realize how much I depended on her. In a lot of ways she's all I have." Wiping her moist eyes with the back of her hand, she glanced away. He moved up onto the perch beside her in one motion. The bucket of apples was relegated to the paint holder on the ladder. A comforting arm was placed around her shoulders.

"I'm sorry I upset you." He sighed wearily, the warmth of his body against her side soothing. "I should have asked your permission before auditioning Amy, regardless of what she told me." He looked away, mouth taut. "Maybe on some level I knew that there was some justification for your anger when you came to my suite. For a long time my filmmaking has been all I had, too—I put everything into it. Sometimes I unintentionally let the personal considerations of others come last. I won't do that again. I've promised myself I'll be more aware."

Colleen had the feeling he already had. "Peace?" he questioned quietly.

She smiled her forgiveness and extended her hand. "Peace." Lyon moved from his perch on the tree, to the ladder, gave her a hand down. "So what are you doing out here all alone?" he asked. Colleen dusted off the back of her jeans once her feet hit the ground.

"I came out to check on the property, spend some time alone." It had disturbed her to realize that despite her pique with Lyon, she had been neither able to entirely dismiss nor forget him. Maybe it was because he was different from any other man she had ever known. Or maybe there was something more about him that drew her, something she wasn't yet able to face.

"Nice place," Lyon commented, looking around admiringly.

She nodded, supplying the information, "We own sixty acres here, but most of the fields are fallow."

"Amy said the farm had been in your family for generations."

"Yes. It's the last link I have with my parents. There are times we could have used the money—especially when it came to meeting the costs of putting Amy through college—but I've been reluctant to sell it."

The house was situated well back from the road, in a grove of walnut and hickory trees, hidden from view. When the farm was unoccupied, a heavy chain and double-locked gate and No Trespassing sign kept strangers out.

He gestured toward the curl of woodsmoke rising from the chimney. "Are you staying at the house?"

She nodded. "Overnight. I've got some paperwork to get caught up on."

He folded the ladder for her and tucked it under his arm while she picked up the basket of apples. "The phone works, you know. You could have called. Amy and I like to come up here weekends and holidays, whenever we can, so we leave the utilities turned on."

"Amy mentioned that, but the truth is I wanted to see you. I wanted to talk to you yesterday but there were too many people around." She turned a questioning glance his way. "I've got the rest of the day off. I was hoping we could spend the evening together." It was a simple invitation, issued out of friendship as much as anything else. She wanted his companionship, she realized.

"Would you like to stay for dinner?" she asked impulsively. "I've got plenty."

He hesitated, his eyes searching her face. "You're sure it wouldn't be too much trouble. We could go out."

"Dinner's already started." He'd made such an effort, the least she could do was meet him halfway. Together they returned the ladder to the barn. Companionably they walked toward the house.

The delicious smell of roasting meat and spices filled the country kitchen. "Can I get you something to drink?" Colleen asked. In the living room a fire burned in the grate. The spacious room was painted white and had a red brick floor. There was a scarred, bleached oak table and chairs in the same light-colored wood.

"A glass of wine would be nice," he replied with a warm smile.

During dinner they chatted amicably. He told her about his past films. She told him about her life with her folks, more about her life since. They did the dishes together, working like a practiced team, then ventured into the living room and drank coffee before the fire. He glanced at his watch—nearly midnight. She wondered fleetingly where the time had gone.

"I should be going." He stood. "Is there a hotel nearby?"

"There are several on the interstate. None as luxurious as the penthouse suite at the Regency Hotel, but they're all okay as far as accommodations go." She added sympathetically, "It is a long drive back to the city." She moved to get the jacket he had brought with him, nervous now that the moment to say good-night had come. "How long did it take you to get up here?" She turned and found herself confronted with the solid wall of his chest.

He took his suede jacket from her hands, his fingertips brushing hers lightly. "About two and a half hours. I took a wrong turn near Bellefontaine."

"Oh. Some of these country roads aren't very well marked. Were the directions Amy gave you okay?"

"Yes."

He paused, his gaze as darkly seductive and waiting as his stance. They'd run through all the pleasantries. More than once he had thanked her for the home-cooked meal, the apple pie she had hurriedly baked, with his help, for dessert. It was time for him to leave, and yet...she had never wanted anything more in her life than for him to stay. The hypnotic tone of his voice, the dark yearning intent in his eyes all combined to disturb yet draw her to him compellingly. He was feeling the attraction, too. He wanted to reach out and embrace her, wanted to touch her as much as she craved touching him.

"I don't want to go." He tossed his jacket to the side.

There was no pretending she didn't feel the same. "I know," she admitted quietly. She could hear the cadence of his breathing and her pulses pounding like primitive drumbeats in her ears. "But I can't ask you to stay here, Lyon. It's too soon."

"Is it?" he disagreed quietly. "I think I've known from the very first how I felt about you, what I wanted." His eyes were darker, more intense, than she had ever seen them.

At his velvet-rough tone, muscles tightened deep inside her. Fear, the age-old tension between man and woman, strength and weakness, flooded her senses, her heart. And anticipation at discovering the mysterious sensuous side of him. "Lyon—"

He gave her no more chance to resist him, taking her tenderly into his arms in a possession of the most insidious kind. He seemed to think they could sort it all out later, that the only thing important now was to take and to give, to feel and to love. And, heaven help her, she wanted all that and more. He took her lips, the inside of her mouth, the fiery caress all liquid movement and controlled passion, inundated with the need to give as well as to receive. It was a hunger that spoke to her soul and sent the last walls of her reserve tumbling down as he asked everything of her and pledged, with his loving gestures, everything in return.

His hands traced the contours of her body through the fabric of her dress, pleasuring the soft globes of her breasts with the insistent motions of his fingertips, his palms moving restlessly over the planes of her back, whisper-soft strokes down the long column of her spine, ending at the delicate hollow of its base. "I want to touch you here." His hands traveled lightly across her waist. "And here." His thumb pressed down in the flowering moistness between her thighs. "And here." His hands cupped her buttocks, cradling her against the swelling pressure of his desire.

"I want to see the glow of firelight on your skin." A shudder of arousal and anticipation swept through her, weakening her knees. Masterfully he maneuvered her until the backs of her thighs touched the uncluttered surface of a sturdy rectangular writing table where she gratefully sat.

His legs shifted until he was standing astride her, girding and trapping her slender thighs in the sinewy cradle of his strong limbs. One large hand swept behind her, throwing her slightly off balance so she had to cling to his shoulders. He moved with her, his face hungry, delighting in her spontaneous response.

The buttons of her blouse were unfastened; he moved the cloth from her shoulders, watching as it pooled at her waist. "You're beautiful," he murmured, his eyes glowing warmly as he traced the satiny flesh spilling above the lacy cups of her brassiere.

Deftly he released the back clasp of her bra. The restrictive cloth slid from her arms, leaving her open to his rapt gaze. Instinctively, shyly, she moved a forearm as if to cover herself from chill air and his gaze. "Don't," he whispered softly, fiercely, gently capturing her elbow and moving her arm to her side. "I want to see you." His stubble-roughened cheek pressed intimately against the softness of her breast. "Kiss you. Taste you. Sweet, so sweet," he murmured against her pounding heart. His face moved into the deep valley between her breasts. Tremors of arousal shook her as he breathed in her musky perfume, then touched the tip of his tongue to that which he had inhaled. Each hot wet kiss on her breasts left her throbbing with delight. In slow languid sweeps he pressed tiny love bites into her skin, tantalizing her further into ecstasy, then with soft sweeping licks of his tongue, healed that which needed no healing. His thumbs brushed her nipples repeatedly, until she could do little more than gasp at the searing turmoil inside.

"Let me love you," he whispered. He brushed his lips along her cheek until they met her mouth in a kiss that made Colleen shudder with renewed longing. Satiation that only he could give was just moments away. But he wanted to hear her give her permission. "Colleen?"

His voice, more impatient now, more serious, more demanding, acted like a warning bell on her already overloaded senses. With effort she dragged her attention from the sensual whirlpool he had created between them. Meeting his gaze, she yearned to discover fully the passionate tenderness she saw reflected in the amber depths. But the thought of the temporariness of their liaison cast the first doubt into the wellspring of longing in her heart. And with that action came the fading of her ardor.

Reading her decision, he abruptly turned away. The silence that fell was a gap of regret neither could bridge. Mortified by the ease with which she had almost given herself to him, Colleen fumbled with her clothing, with difficulty managed to retrieve and slip into her bra. With trembling fingers, aware of his steady, measuring gaze, she slid the long soft sleeve of her cotton shirt over her arms.

"What happened to make you change your mind?" he asked at last. Though not touching her, he was standing in front of her, so close as to make escape impossible. Whatever resentment he'd initially felt had faded, to be replaced by a thorough contemplation she found even more disturbing.

I realized you don't love me, she thought. That in the end this affair would be meaningless, to him. And probably for her, all too brief and because of what he did not feel, emotionally unfulfilling. She turned her head to the side, letting the curtain of her silky hair shield her face. "As I said, it was happening too fast."

His hand touched her chin, increasing the pressure until she obeyed his wish and lifted her face to his. His gaze was clouded with an emotion she couldn't decipher. "Too fast or too freely?" His mouth tightened, whether in irritation at himself or with her she couldn't tell. She didn't reply. His hand dropped. "You're the kind of woman who needs commitment," he observed. "I shouldn't have started anything." Chill regret dominated his tone.

"We shouldn't have started anything," she corrected quietly. She couldn't have been seduced if she hadn't wanted to be. Perhaps it was that knowledge of the desire hidden within her that bothered her most.

Sensing the extent of her dismay, Lyon stood stock-still in the center of the room. "Colleen..." He obviously wanted to comfort her but didn't know where to begin.

"It's late. Just go."

"All right." Reluctantly he left. The last image she had was of the guilt on his face. It haunted her for the rest of the night.

8

"JUST ONE MORE PAGE of figures from the ledger to input and I'll be done." Colleen sighed with relief. Bookkeeping was a chore she tolerated but did not like. Fingertips poised over the computer keyboard, she leaned toward the terminal screen.

Footsteps echoed in the outer hall, followed by the sound of the front door opening and closing. Assuming it was either Blake or Pansy coming into the salon, Colleen continued typing in figures, only swiveling her chair around toward the door when the footsteps neared her work area. Beyond her cubbyhole of an office, the interior of the salon glistened from the recent weekend cleaning. Seconds later Lyon Haggerty appeared in the doorway. He was wearing a safari-style jacket, matching khaki trousers and a soft-looking print shirt. The whole outfit was impeccably fitted to his muscular form.

Suddenly, her heart was thudding in her chest. Her hands were wet with perspiration, and she found herself holding her breath. He had never looked cooler, more composed.

She didn't know which disturbed her more, his elemental sensuality or the innate gentleness in his steady regard. She felt she could succumb to either trait. They murmured polite hellos, but Colleen remained in her swivel chair, facing him curiously. "How did you get in?" Because the salon was closed on Sundays, she had locked the door after entering.

He handed over a key, his hand brushing hers. "Amy generously lent me this. She thought you might not hear me knock from back here." The way he looked at her told her he was recalling their steamy goodbye kiss. Colleen ran a hand through her hair, automatically smoothing the ends. She was dressed casually in faded jeans, an oversize blue, pink and lavender plaid shirt with a snapped-up cowl neck and three-quarter sleeves. Nonetheless his appraisal was openly admiring, raising her temperature decidedly. Body heat, she thought, his and hers.

Colleen was the first to look away. She busied herself straightening the stack of papers and the ledgers that were spread out over the computer console and her desk.

Appearing perfectly content and relaxed, he leaned one hip on the edge of her desk. "Aren't you curious as to what else Amy and I talked about?"

Colleen paused, a sheaf of papers in her hands. "How is Amy?"

"Talkative as usual." He grinned, then became more serious. "She said you sounded a little down this morning when you called to let her know you were back in the city. I'm sorry if I came on too strong last night," Lyon finished gently, turning a small notepad over and over. He was making no attempt to conceal his emotions, but that didn't make it any easier for her to read them.

She became officious again, needlessly straightening various objects on her desk. "Do we have to talk about this?"

"No, but I want to." His expression was frank and beguiling. When she held his look, he said softly, "I forget sometimes that not everyone lives moment to moment. If I offended or upset you, I am sorry. That was never my intention."

Heat suffused her face as their eyes met. She wanted to believe what was beginning to happen between them was special. "But you do live moment to moment?"

"I have been lately, yes." He paused. "But being around you, I'm beginning to see that could change."

Her heart lifted a little at his confession. Needing time to absorb what he had just said, she rose, putting a ledger back on a shelf above her filing cabinet.

His gaze followed her and he asked casually, "What are you doing here on a Sunday?"

"Bookkeeping, a little inventory."

He frowned as she turned back to him. The mesmeric eyes held her in a tantalizing embrace. She could comfortably drown in their amber-flecked depths, she thought irrelevantly.

"Don't you hire people to do your books?"

She shrugged. "It's silly to hire someone when I have a computer to work for me. I only hire someone at tax time."

He responded gruffly, "You should have someone doing that for you; you work hard enough as it is."

She laughed, glad to get the conversation back onto safer ground. "Now you sound like Amy."

"In this one instance your sister is right."

She smiled, warmed by his concern. "Was there any particular reason you stopped by?"

His teeth flashed white in a broad, persuasive smile. "It's a gorgeous day and I thought you might enjoy it with me. I want us to be together."

She sensed that he had more than just casual conversation and companionship on his mind. To be perfectly honest, she had to admit to wanting more, too. Justifiably wary about where an afternoon of togetherness might lead, she turned him down with a shake of her head. She had made a fool of herself the evening before, backing out at the last moment. She wouldn't do it again. "I'm sorry. Thank you for asking, but I can't. I've got to finish my paperwork."

He sent her a level look, as if to inform her he knew very well why she wouldn't go with him, then shrugged. Settling himself in a chair opposite her desk, he crossed his long legs, one ankle over the other bent knee, and made a steeple of his fingers. "It's still early. I can wait."

A steely, stubborn determination, honed by years of self-reliance, lifted her chin as she warned politely, "You're in for a long afternoon, Lyon. If I'm to work on your set tomorrow morning as a consultant, I've got to finish my accounting and inventory now. I still have a lot of work to do."

He was studying her closely, but he didn't comment on the circles of fatigue under her eyes, other than to say, "You have other people working for you. Couldn't they do it?"

Colleen wouldn't admit how tired she was; that she'd lost sleep over Lyon the night before and then been up at the crack of dawn, feeling restless and irritable and at odds with even herself. "It's my business," she said firmly. "I prefer to keep track of it myself."

Her devotion to her work he could accept. "Okay, then, since it's my fault you have to work so much overtime this week, I'll pitch in, too. We'll consider it a favor for a favor. How can I help you?" He rolled up his sleeves.

She stared at him in bewilderment, her pique fading. "You're serious."

"Quite."

In the end she decided it would be easier just to accept his offer than to spend the rest of the day arguing. She soon had him counting bottles of shampoo, conditioner, different types of colors and perms, while she compared his findings against the normal monthly usage. Using the computer, she quickly tallied the data and figured out what to order. The whole process took several hours, even with the two of them working. He was on his best behavior—businesslike and cool the entire time. Conversely, Colleen felt as if she'd been hanging upside down on a Ferris wheel, her emotions were in such a jumble. After the passion that had sizzled between them the evening before, she was unable to decide whether his attitude pleased or disappointed her.

A companionable silence fell between them, generated by their joint effort, but Colleen had the uncomfortable feeling that she was skirting dangerously close to an emotional minefield. To want, to fear, to give, to love—that was the progression of passion, and she was treacherously close to succumbing. And Lyon seemed to know it.

"Well? Don't I deserve something for all my hard work?" Despite his softly seductive tone, his look was all innocence. Again she felt her defenses crumbling.

"Like what?" Involuntarily, she warmed to his lighthearted mood.

"Like that outing I was trying to talk you into earlier?"

Her lips curved into a reluctant, exasperated smile. "What did you have in mind?"

He grinned victoriously. "I thought we'd drive up to Buckeye Lake."

Buckeye Lake, though serene and relatively undeveloped and unspoiled, was not exactly the hot spot of the Midwest. "And do what?"

He raised both hands, palm up, in a careless gesture. "Talk. Get to know each other better."

Alarm bells sounded in her head. "I won't put the moves on you, if that's what you're thinking." His voice was serious but calm. He had read her thoughts but wasn't offended.

She knew how very little willpower she had when it came to resisting, but his earlier kindness had already decided her. "Let me get my jacket."

He had a picnic basket in his car.

"Confident, weren't you?"

He grinned. "Yes."

She stole glances at him as he drove out to the lake. He looked happy and composed, his hands masterfully circling the wheel, and his ebullient mood was contagious. Once there, they selected a grassy spot at the edge of a grove of trees, high on a bluff overlooking the lake. It was a perfect autumn afternoon—crisp, sunny, quiet. Peace stole over her. And gladness, gladness that she had come here with him, that he had returned even after the disaster of the evening before. Could it be he was beginning to care about her, too?

"A loaf of Italian bread, French pastries, Belgian chocolates, specially blended Colombian coffee, Danish ham, English crackers, French Brie and Swiss cheese, Dom Perignon champagne. Is this a picnic lunch or a United Nations celebration?"

Laughing, he brought out a delectable assortment of plums, grapes, oranges, apples and pears. "Don't forget the fruit from California."

"Ah, yes, the good old United States of America, too." The elaborate wicker hamper also contained not paper plates, but china, silver, crystal and Irish linen.

The day drifted pleasurably. After eating their fill they lounged on the blanket, not touching, yet somehow replete just laughing, talking.

"You really like running your own business, don't you?" he observed after a while.

"Oh, yes." Colleen nodded enthusiastically. "It beats working for someone else hands down."

"It's a lot of work, a lot of responsibility."

"Freedom, too, though." She paused, pleating a corner of the blanket between her fingers. "The pleasures and satisfaction far outweigh the disadvantages."

"I can see how it would give you satisfaction." He brooded, then, staring out at the glimmering surface of the lake. "What would happen if you were to marry, though? Would you maintain your business?" His eyes met hers. Much seemed to hinge on her answer.

Colleen answered thoughtfully, honestly, "I can't imagine not working, though I'd try to achieve a balance between work and home, and hope my husband—if I ever marry—would understand."

Lyon nodded. She wasn't sure he agreed with or even understood her point of view. Curious, she asked, "What happened to your first marriage?"

Lyon stretched out beside her, unhappiness and resignation reflected on his face. "The strain of living apart most of the time finally took its toll. Marilyn is a producer for a news show on public television. Her work kept her from traveling with me on location. You can't build much of a marriage if you're never together." There was an underlying note of bitterness in his voice.

"Was that the only reason you divorced?"

"She didn't trust me to be faithful to her." The bitterness was more pronounced.

Infidelity Colleen could not forgive, either. "Were you unfaithful?"

"I never slept with anyone else when we were married, never even thought about it," Lyon answered brusquely. He sighed heavily. "I suppose what bothered me most was her lack of faith. She didn't trust me not to hurt her, didn't believe in me to do the right thing where others were concerned."

Colleen knew then how hurt Lyon must have been by the way she had reacted to his hiring Amy for his film. No wonder he had been angry. Prior to that he had given her no reason to think he would act so terribly, yet she'd leaped to that conclusion nonetheless. "Are you still in love with your ex-wife?" She asked quietly—something seemed to be bothering him.

"No. I was very much in love with her when we met, but she's a different woman now, a stranger." Someone he didn't even seem to like, Colleen observed. She tightened her hand beneath his. "The marriage is over, Colleen; it has been for a long time."

That, she could believe. What she didn't understand were the expectations he held about future romantic involvements. "Would you expect a woman you're involved with to give up her work?"

Carefully he replied, "No, but I would want the woman I fall in love with to put us first and not her work."

About that much, he was adamant.

By the time they arrived back at the Trendsetter, darkness was falling. He walked her as far as her car. "Thanks for a lovely afternoon." She touched his arm, her palm resting on the hard swell of muscle beneath his coat.

"I enjoyed it," he said softly.

The cool outdoor air was heated by the warmth of his breath, mingling with hers. There was nothing intense about his expression. It represented friendship and a certain easygoing amusement. Disappointment flooded her. This was it, then, another evening come to an end, a relatively good time had by all but nothing in the future, nothing to be gained by it happening again, except maybe heartache and pain.

"I wish you wouldn't look at me like that," he said softly. "It makes me feel—"

He broke off, the evening shadows etching stark lines into his face as he recognized the yearning deep within her. Gathering her into his arms, he held her snugly against his hard length, then bent to take her lips with his own.

Parting her lips, she wreathed her arms about his neck, needing his warmth, his gentleness more than ever before. His mouth moved over the softness of her cheek, the column of her neck, savoring every touch as she simultaneously savored him. The flavor of his skin, the scent of his after-shave, the velvet of his mouth when contrasted with the faint sandpapering of his evening beard against the smoothness of his skin, all combined to urge her close against him. Hardness to softness, intense, male....

"Colleen," he murmured her name softly, once, and then again.

Her hands slid under his jacket, pressed against his spine. She loved the way her body fit so perfectly with his and then he shifted with a sensuous roll of his hips, giving her even greater pleasure. He kissed her slowly, thoroughly, evoking sensation after delicious sensation.

When at last the embrace drew to a lingering halt, her emotions were whirling. She felt as if she had been transported on a soft and wispy cloud, and for a moment she had lost sight of reality. He drew her to him again, kissing her gently one last time before she realized it really was time for her to go.

He waited while she found her key, inserted it into the lock, slid behind the wheel of her car. The door shut. *I'm insane*, she thought, *certifiably insane to be playing so willingly with fire*.

Watching him walk off without a backward glance, she knew full well Lyon would dominate her dreams, not just this night, but every other, if she lived to be one hundred and one years old. Like it or not, she had fallen in love with him.

9

COLLEEN STOOD in the shadows of the movie set, watching the crew as they arranged the furniture and props for the next scene. It was difficult to believe she had been working here for nearly three full days, they had passed so quickly. During that time she had come to realize that she wasn't alone in her affection for Lyon; everyone involved with this project seemed to respect and admire him. His appeal was never more evident than when he was very much involved in his work, as he was at the moment.

A few feet away, Lyon blocked the scene, emphatically reminding the young actors of the importance of their movements on stage. "You've got to be constantly aware of the camera, making sure you're in the right place, at the right time, kids. An inch off the mark and you're out of the shot. Every element must be perfectly timed and coordinated or we have nothing."

A utilitarian gray sweatshirt molded the contours of his chest; soft faded jeans hugged his lean hips. A black director's cap, emblazoned with Hearts in Jeopardy, was pushed back on his head, the dark fabric a contrast to the tousled gold disarray of his hair.

Colleen waited patiently until he had finished and caught him a moment later, before the filming began. "Lyon, I've got to go. I'm needed at the salon."

"Sure?"

"Yes. My time on the set has been fun. It was a marvelous challenge, trying to create exactly the right 'look' for such a diverse group of people. And I've never been better received, either by the makeup technicians I've assisted creatively or the actors I've worked with."

Lyon's expression softened as he removed his hat and raked a hand through his hair. There were waves where the cap had sat. "Thanks for giving us as much time as you did. We couldn't have done it without you."

"I'm glad I could help. But my job is done. Your regular technicians can take it from here." Although the days spent on his set had been exhilarating, it was time to get back to her own business. She couldn't keep relying on others to do her job for her at the Trendsetter.

"I'm going to miss having you here," he confided, his eyes searching her own, lingering on her face.

"I'll miss being here. But rather than stay on and be bored, I want to get back to my shop."

His expression was regretful. "Unfortunately, I probably won't be able to see you for a while. My schedule for the next few days is hectic."

She knew how busy he had been and still would be.

"I understand." Her throat was aching, dry. "I'll miss seeing you, too."

"I'll call you when I can," he promised.

"I'll be thinking of you." She managed a smile.

They parted on that pledge.

Every night that week they talked and at odd moments throughout the days, looking forward to a weekend they had agreed to spend together. On Friday gifts began to arrive.

First was an orchid, with a note that read, "You're a woman who belongs in silks and black velvet. I want to give you those things and much much more." It was signed simply *L*.

Second was a stunning floor-length black velvet dress, long-sleeved and V-necked, with the enclosed card, "Nothing could be softer than your skin."

"I'm beginning to like this," Blake said, watching as she folded the lovely designer gown back into the tissue-wrapped box. Her cheeks were stained scarlet, Colleen knew.

"Me, too." Pansy popped her gum, teasing curiously, as she moved closer, her spike-heeled thigh-high boots tapping a staccato rhythm on the floor. "What'd the letter say, Colleen?"

Colleen hedged, "He wants me to have something nice to wear." It was as close a translation as they were going to get. She folded the note and placed it in her pocket.

Thinking the parade of gifts was over, everyone went back to work, but after lunch came a beautiful strand of pearls and matching earrings in a black velvet case. A uniformed chauffeur delivered them.

A bottle of ultra-expensive specially blended perfume from Giorgio's of Beverly Hills followed. "The closest I could come to the delicate scent of your skin," the enclosed card stated.

At the salon staff's prodding, Colleen once again carefully paraphrased the note, "He wants me to smell good."

"I'll say!" Pansy exclaimed. "The man is totally awesome and I mean totally! Far out!" She peered myopically at Colleen. "Say, does he have any brothers? Cousins? I'll settle for a distant relative."

Combing out his client's soft waves, Blake remarked, "That's a man with love on his mind, if I ever saw one."

Delicate glittery black pumps and a matching evening bag from an exclusive Rodeo Drive establishment were delivered next. The card read, "I've missed you. See you tonight? I'll send a car to your place at seven."

Filled with dreams of their evening together, Colleen was just closing up the shop at five-thirty, eager to be on her way home, when the phone rang. Reluctantly, she answered it. "Hi," she said in response to Lyon's cheery hello.

Oh, please don't let anything go wrong with tonight! she thought.

"You received the gifts?"

"Yes, I did. Thank you. They're lovely." She sensed something was wrong when he didn't say anything else immediately. "You're not canceling our date?" she questioned warily.

Regret tinged his voice as he admitted, "We've got a problem here on the set. One of the scenes simply isn't working. We're going to have to rewrite it and refilm it next week. I've got to go to Los Angeles to meet with the screenwriter who did the initial screenplay."

"When?" Trepidation underscored her voice.

"Tonight."

Damn! "Couldn't the writer come to Ohio instead?"

"Afraid not. Not this time." About that much, he was firmly insistent.

"Look, I know it's short notice," he hurried on before she could speak. "But I'd like you to come with me if you can. It would give you a chance to see my place in Bel Air. I promise I'll make up for the hassle and change of plans tomorrow evening with something very special."

The invitation to go away for the weekend was casually extended, yet she knew in her heart to accept would very likely mean that in the process they would become lovers. It was what she wanted, she realized. And even if it hadn't been, she knew him well enough to realize there would be no pressure, sexual or otherwise, the days on the set had proved that. If and when it happened that they did make love, it would be her decision. She cherished the freedom he had given her most of all. The chance to be with him obliterated all else. Her spirits soared. "I'd love to go," she decided finally.

"Great! I'll pick you up at your place in an hour. Our flight leaves Columbus at seven-thirty. We arrive in Los Angeles at eleven forty-five Pacific time."

"I'll be ready."

His laughter was husky, warming her to her very soul. "Oh, and Colleen, be sure to bring the presents I sent you. We'll make good use of them tomorrow night."

UPON ARRIVAL, Lyon gave Colleen a tour of his home. It was luxurious, as she had expected, tastefully decorated in an eclectic combination of both new and old.

"Tired?" he asked as he carried her bags to the guest room. One suitcase contained the belongings she'd packed, the other his gifts.

"No." She'd never felt more elated or less like sleeping, though the flight had been a long one. They'd been met at the airport by paparazzi, some of whom Lyon recognized from the notoriously inept and inaccurate supermarket scandal sheet *Star Time*.

His eyes met hers. His gaze held a distinctly sensual message—a message she was powerless to ignore or avoid. Then he smiled and said, "I'd like a glass of wine before we turn in. Will you join me?" He leaned one shoulder against the wall, watching her, and at that moment saying yes seemed suddenly dangerous, yet more tempting than anything that had gone before in her life.

"Yes." Her throat was dry as his gaze lingered on the outline of her breasts beneath her midnight-blue silk dress. She wasn't wearing a bra, and she knew he could tell.

Arm around her waist, he escorted her into the library. Wordlessly he led her to the rug before the fire. Throw pillows were tossed on the floor. The lights were dimmed, the setting romantic. They shared a glass of wine, and then without speaking, he was urging her down, stretching out beside her. His look was so ardent, it sent a tremor through her. The brisk scent of his cologne blended intoxicatingly with the freshly soaped scent of his skin. He kissed her lingeringly, with an erotic tenderness that made her shiver. The hem of her dress had twisted up past her calves to her knees. With a deliberate sweeping motion of his palm he eased it up past her waist, over her shoulders. It floated in a circle onto the floor, leaving her achingly vulnerable to his touch, his gaze. "You're so lovely," he whispered, his breath hot against her ear.

"Touch me, Lyon, please. Touch all of me."

A low moan sounded in his throat. He paused, then clasped her to him, his breath uneven against her cheek. Capturing handfuls of her hair, he held her mouth beneath his, his lips savoring and instructing on all the ways they could kiss. His hands caressed the satiny softness of her thighs, then moved to her breasts, circling, lightly teasing the rosy crests. She strained to meet his cupping palms, wordlessly telling him of her arousal. He bent and kissed first one taut nipple, then the other, then rolled slightly, so that one of his thighs was nestled securely between hers, holding her still. "God help me, I want you," he said hoarsely. "But not...too fast. Not this fast."

Slowly she worked her way down the buttons of his shirt, unfastening, then spreading wide each giving section of cloth. "I want you, too." Her splayed fingertips coasted sensually down his chest to his waist. His eyes above her were liquid, shimmering, intense.

Raising her arms, she ran her hands over his broad shoulders, his strong back, loving the feel of toned muscle and warm flesh. Then, locking one hand over the other, she held his head for her kiss, while her fingertips plowed through the silky softness of his wheat-colored hair. Her tongue slid past the barrier of his teeth, touching his tongue.

"I want to give you pleasure," she breathed, her open mouth tracing the evening beard that shadowed his chin. He trembled slightly, and his shudder of arousal sent new anticipation tumbling through her veins.

"And what else do you want?" His arms twined around her back, tightening until she could barely breathe. His fingers were hot on her skin. She moaned and arched against him, her feminine contours molding to his masculine form. His hands spread her thighs, as he pressed more deeply, wantonly, against her until she moaned with pleasure. Then, increasing the pressure, he held still until she was all wildfire, pure passion and need.

Love, she thought, *I want your love*. But the words were lost with the slow descent of his mouth upon hers. And then there was only his mouth touching hers, tasting, tormenting. She arched against him, wanting only to feel closer, to be naked, skin to skin. As if reading her mind, he moved away from her. They finished undressing each other slowly, with care.

The discarded clothes and pillows formed a makeshift bed as he positioned her beneath him once more. Heat and need suffused her. Her splayed fingers raked down his chest, past his waist, then curved up his spine, to his shoulders, finally lower, to his flanks, the innermost surface of his thighs.

"You feel...so good," he murmured, touching his lips to hers. His hands swept down between their bodies, caressing her with tantalizingly slow strokes, tracing every indentation, every hollow, every sweet soft petal of her femininity.

Murmuring helplessly, she trailed her fingers downward, tantalizing him with gentle strokes, reveling in his maleness. Then, feeling his reaction, she shifted onto her back, her arms and legs both wrapped around his waist, drawing him down against her.

Holding her head he plundered her mouth with his tongue, impatience and tenderness mingling in the masterful caress. His free hand moved beneath her, lifting her, cupping her to him. His legs, all corded-muscle strength, spread and then pressed against her open thighs. While his mouth covered hers with kisses his fingers found and traced her center. She arched against him convulsively, once, twice, feeling her body open for him as completely and unselfishly as her heart, and then he was inside her, all hot, rhythmic male insistence. Clinging to him, she gave him the response he sought, knowing no limitations, no inhibitions. The world spun away on a whirlwind of delicious sensations and then there was only passion, the whisper of her name and his echoing in the night.

They lay cozily entwined before the fire. She wanted to remember him this way forever, splendidly naked, wrapped in her arms, his hair all tousled, eyes glowing amber.

His arms tightened around her possessively as he whispered, "There will be no one else for me from this moment on." His lips met hers. Before she could speak, he again showed her the many ways they could love.

Colleen awakened the next morning in Lyon's bed, remembering how passionate Lyon's lovemaking had been, how uninhibited her own response. She stretched, turning over to revel in the pampering luxury of silk sheets and further take in her surroundings. The spacious master bedroom was as elegant and expensively outfitted as the rest of the house. A silver-and-gold Chinese print papered the walls; the bed was draped in a luxurious ivory satin spread. For the moment, heavy quilted draperies blocked out the sun. The pillows beside her were empty, as was the rest of the room. Vaguely she recalled Lyon's mentioning something about his appointments with writers starting early.

Rising, she shrugged into a robe, and went into the adjoining bath. Later, showered, dressed, every hair in place, she ventured downstairs to find him.

Lyon was in the living room with screenwriter Marcy Dalton. Her petite figure blossoming in the last stage of her pregnancy, Marcy was lovely and reassuringly genial as Lyon made introductions. After the women had exchanged greetings he informed, "Marcy wrote the original screenplay for *Hearts in Jeopardy*. Her husband is an executive at the studio where I do my films." A roomy rectangular custom-built sofa dominated the sunken conversation pit. A beautiful tapestry unified the subtle neutral color scheme of the room and a variety of plants, naturally finished oak end tables and modern sculptures completed the luxurious center of the impressive hillside residence.

"Not that my husband's position gives me an edge over other writers competing for the chance to have their screenplays produced," Marcy groaned. "I have to work twice as hard as anyone else, just to be acknowledged."

"Which brings us to the next point," Lyon said sternly. "Should you be working when it's so close to your due date? You know we could easily hire another writer to fill in on this one scene, without taking any credits away from you."

Marcy laughed. "Listen to him. Just because he's the godfather to be...." Tone softening, she reassured him, "It's not as if we haven't done this before, Lyon. Nick and I are old hands at bringing a baby into this world." To Colleen, she explained, "We have a three-year-old son, Peter." She turned back to Lyon. "Stop worrying! I'll be fine!"

At her passionate disclaimer, Lyon's eyes narrowed. Colleen leaned back amused. She'd seen him mother over the people who worked on the movie set, too. "How close are you to being due to deliver?" she asked.

Marcy shrugged. "A couple of days."

"See what I mean about cutting it close?" He turned to Colleen, as if for backup in his concern over the writer's health and that of her unborn child.

"I'll be fine," Marcy reiterated.

Lyon made a noise in his throat that sounded like harumph, shaking his head in obvious disapproval. "You know, Marcy, you and Nick may have forgotten all the chaos that went on the last time you two had a baby, but I certainly haven't!" He turned to Colleen, explaining, "Nick was frantic and bumbling his every responsibility. Marcy wouldn't even leave for the hospital until the pains were four minutes apart." There was something like envy in his tone.

Marcy shrugged off her past behavior. "I had a scene to finish writing, Lyon. It was in my head. I had to put it on paper. Otherwise I never would have been able to concentrate on my LaMaze."

"No literary heroics this time, promise?" Lyon turned serious, and Colleen could see his concern for the young woman was genuine.

"Cross my heart. Now. Mind if I use your word processor? Nick's home with Peter—our regular baby-sitter's been battling chronic bronchitis—so there's no telling how long they'll last before sending up the SOS. Which, by the way, I firmly plan to ignore until I complete my work." To Colleen, she explained, "Lyon and I have compatible computers. It saves time. That way we don't have to run back and forth when we're working on such a tight deadline."

Colleen nodded her understanding, genuinely liking the young woman. "Help yourself," Lyon offered graciously. "You know where everything is." Bemoaning both her aching back and the rowdy kicking of the baby, Marcy departed.

Lyon turned to Colleen. "How'd you sleep?" He strode closer.

"Wonderfully."

His gaze fell, taking in her just-showered freshness, the carefully chosen, coral cashmere sweater and white wool slacks. "Had breakfast?"

"No." Her body ached treacherously for contact with his, but he didn't embrace her. Because he was afraid someone else—Marcy, another guest or fellow professional—would stumble in? Or simply because he was reluctant to begin anything he couldn't finish?

"As I said, today will be hectic for me. But I'll make it up to you this evening. In the meantime just make yourself at home."

Her body was already reacting to his nearness— her breasts were peaking beneath the soft coral sweater, a tingling had started in her thighs. But damn it all, he looked so good...she had to stop thinking of that king-size bed just up the stairs.

"If you'd like to borrow a car and go shopping or see some of the sights, there are five cars in the garage. You can take your pick. Just ask Styles for the keys," he added, finishing the routine welcome to his house.

She'd rather have had his time, his attention. But that was impossible. His attempts to find some way to either buy her off or amuse her fell flat. "Maybe I'll just spend some time in the sun," she replied. After all, the Southern California weather was perfect—sunny, warm and breezy.

"Sure? There are tennis courts out back with a machine you can hook up to toss out balls so you can practice your serve. The pool's heated. If you need anything at all, just ask."

Before anything further could be said, the doorbell rang.

Dismissed, she threaded her way through the formal dining room, in search of the kitchen. After a leisurely breakfast Colleen amused herself with an afternoon shopping expedition on Rodeo Drive, where she purchased outrageously sexy lingerie to go with the black velvet dress Lyon had given her.

Lyon met her in the living room upon her return that evening. Colleen glanced around, wondering if—as it looked—they truly were alone.

"Where is everyone?" She tossed her shopping bag on the sofa, ignoring his inquisitive look. His curiosity would have to wait to be sated until she had the provocative garments on.

"Gone." Except for one or two words in passing, Colleen and Lyon had hardly seen each other that morning. Two attorneys, a tax accountant, a set designer for Lyon's next movie and a writer with a script to sell had passed through the house before she had gone out. Doubtless there had been others who appeared, by appointment only, while she had been out killing time.

"Even the housekeeper and butler have left."

Colleen kicked off her shoes and found a comfortable notch in the huge modular sofa that dominated the room. Lyon sat beside her and wordlessly pulled her over, onto his lap. Her arms laced around his neck.

"Today was no way to run a love affair, was it?"

Despite her interest in learning more about the city, the afternoon had been unaccountably tedious. "I admit I would have preferred to see Los Angeles with you at my side," she admitted. "But I still had fun." She'd also seriously contemplated a half-dozen places to open a second Trendsetter. Maybe, just maybe, if she sold the Columbus salon, she could afford to start again. At the very least, to locate in the suburbs. The possibility was more exciting than she had anticipated.

"No more east coast, west coast snobbery?" he teased.

Colleen tried without success to ignore the warm fluttery feeling centered deep inside her. "I'm beginning to see that L.A. could have possibilities for both Amy and myself." For her, the main attraction was Lyon.

His gaze darkened with a warmth that had little to do with desire. "I want to go out for dinner," he urged softly. "Someplace special, where you can wear your pearls and velvet. And to make sure we're not interrupted..." He picked up the cordless phone from the coffee table and dialed his answering service, instructing firmly, "I'll be unavailable for the rest of the night. Hold my messages until tomorrow around—" he cast Colleen a telling look that turned her insides to mush "—noon. Thanks."

The receiver was replaced, his arms tightened around her. "We're all set."

10

"HOW DO YOU LIKE Los Angeles so far?" Lyon asked, drinking in the sight of his dinner companion. She had drawn her hair into a loose topknot, wispy tendrils framing her face. The pearls—heavy and lustrous—lay against her neck, the matching earrings glowed softly in the candlelight. The dress he had purchased for her fit exquisitely, highlighting her slender waist and small high breasts to perfection.

"It's very much like every other big city—busy and exciting. And there's certainly plenty to see and do. The people here seem more laid-back and easygoing than New Yorkers, but I appreciate their warmth and friendliness. Being close to the ocean and beach is a plus, and the weather is wonderful," Colleen enumerated enthusiastically. "It's just cold enough to light a fire at night and, by day it's sunny and warm. The traffic is something else, though."

"Does that bother you?" he asked curiously.

"No, I think I could learn to handle it, as long as I didn't venture out in rush hour until I knew my way around a little better. How cold does it get in winter?"

"I think twenty-eight degrees is our record low." He smiled, capturing her hand with his own. "But generally we have temperate winters. I'm glad you like it here."

She watched him closely. He had promised her an evening to remember and, so far it had been wonderful. "Is it important to you that I like it here?"

He nodded. "It's important."

Not knowing quite what to say, Colleen looked away and glanced around the room. Belgian lace curtains, snowy-white linen, sparkling silver created an aura of Old World charm and serenity. The restaurant was small and intimate, with an open fireplace at one end and large picture windows overlooking the bougainvilleas on the terrace at the other. Bouquets of fresh flowers placed on every table delicately perfumed the air. The lighting was romantically low.

The staff was unobtrusive, yet whenever wineglasses needed filling, the waiter was there. When they had finished with the appetizers of fresh mushrooms marinated in lemon and garlic, he had materialized bearing the next course.

For some time they simply enjoyed the meal, making pleasant, light conversation. Then Lyon seemed to summon up his courage and asked, "Will you be coming to Los Angeles with Amy?"

"She wants me to, and I think I should."

"But you have reservations," he observed astutely.

"I've neglected my business so much during the past few weeks it's a wonder I have any regular customers left at all. If I'm gone for two or three months...well, it's bound to hurt me financially."

"I could get you work here in Los Angeles," Lyon offered. He leaned back slightly to let the waiter take his plate. The main course featured smoked salmon with avocado, sour cream and caviar. "You could certainly work on my film or act as a consultant on any number of others."

"Thank you. I may take you up on that offer."

"Have you ever considered moving to Los Angeles permanently?"

Colleen held her surprise in check. It wasn't like Lyon to pressure a person unduly. "Amy would love that."

"But you wouldn't?" He was watching her steadily, his expression unreadable.

Her finger traced the condensation on her glass of ice water while she thought that, much as she would have liked to be impulsive in her decision, she had to be practical. "I'm not sure it would be the right thing to do. I'd still like Amy to go to college, and she would be more likely to choose that option if we were living in the Midwest."

He didn't argue that point, saying only, "Well, you'll have to make that decision soon. My cast and crew will be leaving Ohio next week."

"You're right. I don't have much time."

Their moods darkened in tandem. Colleen reminded herself firmly that she had known the risks when she went into the affair with Lyon. But she hadn't expected just the thought of never seeing him again to hurt so badly. She had told herself she would just enjoy the moment and then let go. Intellectually, it had seemed to be a plausible idea. After all, they were both adults. Emotionally, though, it wasn't going to be that easy.

Lyon was silent on the drive back to his house. Once inside he steered her into the library. It was the coziest room in the house. Decorated primarily in blue, there were some period pieces and, of course, shelf upon shelf of books. The sofas, upholstered in a sea-shell chintz, were arranged in front of the fireplace over which hung a large landscape by Thomas Cole. It was a beautiful painting of mountain vista and valley, in strong blues and greens. Several old movie posters had been framed and hung on what wall space remained.

"Do you want to tell me what's bothering you?" Lyon asked at last. "Aside from the obvious—the time limitations on our affair." He didn't sound too happy himself.

Colleen kicked off her shoes and curled up in a wing chair, watching as he poured them both snifters of brandy. This was one time when his ability to cut through to the heart of the matter wasn't helping her to open up to him. Yet she owed him an explanation for the downshift in her mood after he had gone to so much trouble to make the evening perfect. She fingered the rope of pearls at her throat.

"I suppose it's the impermanence of everything in my life right now. A few weeks ago Amy and I couldn't have led a more stable, sane existence. Now, I barely know what either of us is going to be doing from day to day. I worry about her future. I worry about mine. I want to stay close to her, but I don't know if I'll be able to do that. Not without sacrificing everything I've built for myself."

He touched her lightly on the arm. "There's nothing selfish about your feelings," he assured her quietly.

So he'd picked up on the guilt in her tone, Colleen thought, and challenged him, "Isn't there?"

"No. You have every right to want things for yourself. You've worked hard to get where you are. Which makes it even harder for me to ask you to leave it."

"Yet you have asked."

"I'm selfish, too," he said in a low voice, his eyes capturing and holding hers for a disconcertingly long time. "Selfish enough to want you all to myself. To want you here."

Lyon was a man who demanded a lot from those around him, who took for granted that he would not be disappointed. Yet she couldn't hold it against him. "I ought to resent you for that."

"But you don't." He leaned back against the bar, and with one hand loosened his tie and the first several buttons of his pleated white shirt.

"No."

He took a swallow of brandy. "Tell me what bothers you most, the impermanence of the move or the impermanence of our relationship?"

Slightly shocked by his bluntness, she nonetheless looked him straight in the eye and answered with equal candor. "Us. I could live with problems in my business. Difficulties in my personal life would be much more unsettling."

Having gone through a divorce, he didn't argue that point. "I had promised myself I wouldn't pressure you. But I can't lie about how I feel, either. I want you to come to Los Angeles."

"So that we might continue to be lovers." She chose her words carefully. She felt as if she were walking in an emotional minefield. If they had lived in the same town, the same state, none of this would have been necessary.

"Yes. But I would have wanted you here in L.A. with me even if we hadn't made love last night, Colleen." He said the words with quiet conviction and her heart soared. "Why not take it one day at a time?" he persuaded softly. "Come to L.A. and see where the future takes us?"

If only it were that easy! she thought despairingly. "A few years ago that would have been fine. But now—"

"You want something more finite, something lasting. You want marriage." There was a faint note of what sounded like contempt in his voice. Then he sighed, obviously searching for a way to explain. "I'm not sure someone in my position should ever be married. I'm on the road a lot, never know from one day to the next what I'll be doing, if we'll be behind schedule on a film or ahead of it. I can't give you a normal nine-to-five life."

She understood that. "Is that the only reason you don't want to marry?" Upon reflection, his speech sounded too well-rehearsed, a smoke screen for inner disillusionment, the painful aftermath of divorce.

"Colleen, I've had marriage. Frankly, I'm not sure it's all it's cracked up to be. My first wife and I promised each other everything and gave each other only pain."

Resentment stiffened her spine. "You're comparing our relationship to what you had with your first wife?"

"I'm saying I can't be sure it would be any different in the long run. And until I am..."

She sighed with relief—he was right. They had only known each other a few weeks. Her posture relaxed by degrees. Wearily she let her head drop forward. Absently, both her hands rubbed at the stiffness in her neck, the result of the tension and anxiety she had been feeling. "Everything is happening so fast. Normally we wouldn't even be discussing such complications at this stage of the romance."

Lyon moved behind her. Aware of her discomfort, he touched a tendril of her hair where it curled against her jaw, then took over the massage of her neck. The pads of his fingers moved in sensual, circular motions at her nape, kneaded her shoulders, brushed lightly at the base of her throat. Lulled by his expert touch, his patient ministrations, she leaned back.

Taking her hand, he moved around the chair and drew her lithely to her feet. "I want us to continue seeing each other." His voice was a husky whisper against her hair.

She turned her head, resting her cheek next to his shoulder, and her senses swam with the contact. "I want that, too." In that moment she realized Lyon had given her more in the short time she had known him than anyone ever had. To continue loving him and be loved in return would be worth the risk of getting hurt.

"Then you'll come?" He sounded so hopeful but still Colleen hesitated.

"I'll consider it. But there's still so much to be worked out. My business—I don't even know if

Blake would be willing to run it for any length of time—"

Eyes darkening, he pulled her closer against him. "Colleen, I love you," he said softly. "I want you to be happy."

"I love you, too." Head against his chest, she felt the steady drumming of his heart.

It seemed like a year since they'd touched. The pressure of his mouth over hers was the sweetest reality. She caught her breath, biting off a low moan of frustration when he stopped and extended his hand to her. Fingers interlaced, they moved silently to the bedroom.

More kisses followed, as soft and silken as his finger tips playing over her flesh. Lyon drew down the zipper of her dress and the velvet fell in a pool at her feet. He groaned, and his hands captured her, all delicate lace and bare skin.

She clung to him, trembling, her lips softening as his kiss turned into flame. Her breasts, which had so longed for his touch, felt the soft sure stroke of his hand as he answered her passion with an achingly gentle touch. His lips moved down her throat, then over her breasts, capturing their tender rosy crests through her filmy bra. His hard thighs urged her softer ones apart until he was pressing into the warm valley between them. And then he removed the rest of her clothing.

Over and over, his fingers stroked her silky inner thighs, stopping just short of the velvet apex between her legs. Unable to control herself any longer, Colleen clutched his shoulders, begging hoarsely, "Please...."

He entered her then, the shock and pleasure of it taking her breath away. Moving in and out of her with long voluptuous strokes, he passionately took control, leading her to fulfillment, to pleasure she had never even imagined...to the shimmering warmth of the sun and the stars...and then there was nothing but his love...his touch...the giving caress of his breath misting her skin as they shuddered convulsively in their mutual release.

He held her against him for a long time afterward, his hands in her hair, sifting through the heavy silk as reverently as if it were the purest gold on earth.

Then, cupping her chin, he tilted her face upward until their eyes met. His were darker, more intense, than she had ever seen them.

"I can take a few days off at the end of next week before we start filming in Los Angeles." Lyon continued softly. "I'd already made plans to spend that time in Switzerland. I want you to go with me, Colleen."

Take it one day, one moment, at a time, she thought. Maybe everything would work out. "Yes, I'll go with you." She knew she would even move to

Los Angeles eventually. But she couldn't help wishing in her heart he had asked her to marry him. The question was, did she have the right to will Lyon to want that, too.

11

"I WANT TO STAY in Los Angeles after my work on *Hearts in Jeopardy* is completed," Amy announced Friday morning as she finished packing. The location work done, she and the rest of the cast and crew were heading for the West Coast, while Colleen and Lyon were getting ready to depart for their Swiss holiday. This was the last time the two sisters would be alone before they both left, and they were spending it readying the condominium for their absence, packing last-minute items and talking heart-to-heart. "I've thought a lot about it and talked to Lyon and Samantha McCreary. They both think it would be good for my career. I could finish high school there, take acting and singing lessons, get an agent, go on auditions...."

"What about college?" Colleen asked, making sure all the windows in Amy's room were securely locked.

"I can take classes at UCLA and use the money I'm getting for working on the film for tuition and living expenses while I get my degree. The best part is I'll be there if any work comes up—hopefully on television or commercials." Amy sat on a suitcase in an effort to close it, found it still half an inch within closing, got up, removed two garments, and tried again. The suitcase latched, but barely. Amy paused. "I wish you'd think about coming west, too. Selling out here, and opening a salon in Los Angeles."

Colleen raked a hand distractedly through her hair, unwilling to admit just how much the possibility had been on her mind already. "You could spend time with Lyon, too," Amy continued to persuade.

"I have been thinking about it," she admitted with a grin.

"That's all I ask," Amy said, giving her sister a hug.

"Come on." Colleen smiled softly. "Let's get you to the airport or we're both going to miss our flights!"

COLLEEN AND LYON'S transatlantic trip was accomplished with amazing ease; his personal secretary had made all the arrangements. After a brief adjustment to the time difference and a recuperative night's sleep, they were ready to see the sights. And see them they did. Their first three days were spent commuting between the fall festivals of Lucerne and Montreux, driving in and out of the mountains, touring quaint villages. By day they tasted wine, reveled in sunshine and crisp autumn weather. Their nights were a blur of happiness and passion. Colleen had never felt so replete, nor so loved.

Nonetheless, every day they were there Lyon received an Air Express package containing business that had to be taken care of immediately. It seemed business was always a part of his life. Or maybe it was just that he was so inordinately successful, there was never any getting away from it, not completely.

They spent their last afternoon touring an old chateau and walking in the mountains. Upon their return, they found that a traditional light supper of fondue, salad and white wine had been prepared and laid out in their absence. Together they cleared away the remains of their meal and the dishes.

While Lyon went through his mail, Colleen placed a call to Amy. "What'd she have to say?" Lyon looked up when Colleen came back into the room minutes later.

"Just that everything is fine. She's looking forward to getting back to filming." Colleen sat on the edge of the couch. "How are things with you?"

He'd been scowling as he glanced through the Air Express package that had arrived in their absence. "As far as the film goes, everything is great. Personally...I'm afraid we've made headlines again."

"What do you mean?" One reason they'd elected to vacation in the remote Swiss village was to avoid the paparazzi. Opening an envelope from his publicist, he informed her matter-of-factly, "We made the 'Stars around Town' column in the latest issue of *Celebrities* magazine." He handed her the clippings.

Of central interest was the photo taken at the Arlington Heights football game. In the picture Colleen seemed to be reeling in a reluctant Lyon to her side. The caption beneath it read, "Colleen Chandler trying to hold on to her man. More than on-location fling?"

So *Celebrities* had doubts, too, she mused, tension lacing its way around her heart. Gamely, she shrugged off the article. "And I thought I had lived that down." She looked at the photo from different angles, remarking cheekily, "Not that it would be so bad if it had been a half-decent picture of me."

"You still would have minded." Lyon commented without looking up.

True, she thought.

"They want to do a story on us," he related, skimming through the accompanying letter bearing the magazine logo.

"Do they want to interview me?" She glanced up in surprise and he nodded his affirmation.

She thought about it for precisely two seconds. "To be truthful, Lyon, one star in the family is enough; I'll leave the posing for publications to Amy." Though not threatened by the interest of the press, Colleen wasn't thrilled, either.

"Is that the only reason? You don't want to undercut Amy's publicity?"

She took a deep breath. "Being branded publically your mistress is not my idea of fun."

"I'm sorry if this bothers you."

"It's my problem, not yours," she assured breezily. But thinking about it further, she had to wonder. Was this what she would be facing if she continued to see Lyon? Could she bear to see their relationship become part of the public domain—everybody's business?

Lyon tossed the papers aside. "I'll tell *Celebrities* no interview. Don't worry about it." He continued flipping through his mail, as if the decision were of no consequence either way. He smiled down at the next clipping in his hand, shook his head ruefully, chuckling, "My publicist must be in seventh heaven. We also made the wire services nationwide in an AP photo of us deplaning in Los Angeles."

Being photographed coming and going, Colleen supposed she could handle though she found it vaguely unsettling to realize that just being with Lyon made her news, too, more so that he enjoyed the exposure. But then she decided that wasn't surprising. Her father had liked being in the spotlight too.

Lyon frowned deeply as he reached for the next item: what appeared to be the cover from a weekly tabloid. "Not so good."

Colleen barely heard him, so intent was she on the cover photo on none other than Pansy's favorite tabloid, *Star Time*. Prominently displayed was a series of photos of herself and Lyon taken on the Bellefontaine farm: Lyon approaching the tree while Colleen calmly continued to pick apples; Lyon moving around the tree to face her; Lyon climbing halfway up the ladder; Colleen sitting perched on a limb, listening unenthusiastically to Lyon talk; Lyon coaxing a reluctant smile from her; both of them in the branches; Lyon's arm around her as Colleen brushed at her tearful eyes; then Lyon moving down the ladder, offering his hand to her. The last photo was the most intrusive of all as it pictured them entering the farm house together at dusk. The caption read, "Lyon Haggerty climbs to new heights of ecstasy with daughter of late senator."

If it hadn't been such an invasion of privacy, it would have been hilarious. To cover her dismay, she observed, tongue-in-cheek, "Well, you can't argue over our placement. Not only did we make the cover, but our story is right there on page two between such scintillating headlines as 'Handicapped Horse Walks Again' and 'The Love That Lost Vigor.'"

One corner of his mouth lifted in a crooked, coaxing smile as he tapped the next page of the tabloid. "Don't overlook 'Princess Di Declares War on Dalmations' or 'Burt Reynolds Says His Beauteous

Ex-girlfriend Was Really A Beast At Heart.' We're up there with all the sought-after celebs."

Colleen pushed herself up from the sofa and paced the room. "No doubt there was someone from the tabloid stalking us from the moment our picture appeared in the Columbus papers."

"Someone must have followed me out to the farm and took those pictures with a telephoto lens," Lyon said quietly. Though not happy about it, he clearly accepted the situation.

She cast the tabloid a disparaging glance. 'The photos are rather grainy, aren't they?"

Soundlessly he got up and poured them each a brandy. "This is very upsetting to you, isn't it?"

"In a sense I feel as if I've been violated," Colleen admitted. Certainly her privacy had been. She gazed at him in despair, then closed her eyes feeling utterly miserable. "You realize that it if someone were there, if they could take pictures of us horsing around and climbing that stupid tree—"

"They could just as easily have been watching us today or any other day." Lyon finished on a taut controlled note.

"What else does it say?"

He put the paper aside, blocking her moves when she tried to reach for it. "Don't worry about it."

"I want to read it. Look, Lyon, if you don't give it to me, I'll simply go out and buy a copy of my own. If not here in Switzerland, then back in the States.

Heaven knows everyone at the salon will have read it. My friends and family, too. How could they not when just standing in line at the store to buy groceries they're bound to see my photograph on the front page?"

His expression grim, Lyon handed the paper to her.

Unhappily, the story reflected all too closely what she felt in her own heart.

Real love or temporary fling? The fairy-tale romance of Lyon Haggerty and salon owner Colleen Chandler is a dream come true, for her at least, all outsiders agree. But friends close to the lovely stylist worry the affair won't last. Since his divorce two years ago, Lyon Haggerty has not been known for his devotion to any woman, having been seen around the world with a great variety of gorgeous young women, most notably and often television and film star Roxanne Stuart. Nevertheless, the newly matched lovebirds have been sighted together at such mundane events as a high-school football game, local pizza parlor, as well as on holiday at the personal residences of Mr. Haggerty in Bel Air and the Chandler family's rustic Ohio farm. No matter what the outcome of the romance, *Star Time* is certain Colleen Chandler will liven up Lyon Haggerty's Ohio stay.

Finished, she handed the paper back to him. Nausea gripped her midsection:

"Would it really bother you so much if the tabloid scrutiny did continue?"

She extricated herself from the loose cradle of his arms and moved away. "I don't know," she said quietly. "The thought of living my life under seige, always looking over my shoulder, wondering if there's a photographer around..." She paused, swallowing hard against the tight knot of emotion in her throat. "When Dad was alive, as members of a senator's family, there was a certain amount of interest paid to us by the press. But it was on a more professional level. Had Amy or I been in trouble with the law or involved in anything unsavory, I guess it would have been different."

Colleen felt the happiness of the sun-kissed day slipping away as the silence stretched between them. Lyon seemed disappointed in her reaction.

"I know you're used to it," she reasoned. "Perhaps in time, I'll be able to adjust, too." In the meantime it was pointless to deny that the unsavory attention given their romance had hurt or that it hadn't stirred up the doubts and turmoil she had been feeling. Was their affair destined to end badly? *Star Time* was correct in stating that Lyon had not been seriously involved with anyone since his divorce. Abruptly she felt the need to get away, to spend some time alone.

She started for the loft of the second floor. "I'm going to take a bath. I'll be down in a while."

He nodded his acknowledgment, something stark and lonely in his eyes. "I've got some calls to make anyway."

Half an hour later, without warning, he appeared in the doorway of the bathroom. She paused in the act of shampooing her hair. He could see her nipples pouting rosily above the frothy white surface of the water. Bubbles glistened incandescently against her skin.

"I've called my attorney," Lyon announced grimly as he walked into the room. "I've instructed him to file suit against the tabloid. They had to have been trespassing on your property when those photos were taken. It won't stop the issue featuring us in that damnable tree from circulating now, but it should curtail their interest in us in the future."

He sat beside the tub. She thought of the unenclosed shower at his home in Bel Air, the relaxation of modesty it encouraged. Tenderly his index finger stroked the slope of her bare shoulder. "I'm sorry that had to happen," he apologized softly. "You have to know if I'd had any idea—"

"It isn't that. Lyon. I just don't want anyone or anything to spoil what we have."

He took over the gentle lathering motions of the shampooing, his fingers gently moving over her scalp. She relaxed under the sureness of his touch, feeling unutterably pampered, content. Beneath the water her limbs had begun to tremble. Though he had kissed her many times through the course of the day, they had yet to make love. Now she wanted him more than ever before.

"No one will." Gently he rinsed the shampoo from her hair, handed her a towel, watched as she fashioned a turban out of the thick powder-blue terry cloth. "I won't let them." He reached for a large bath sheet, also in light blue, and held it open while she stepped into it. Standing silently, bubbles clinging to her body, she luxuriated in the sensation as he gently rubbed her dry. "I've built a fire in the master bedroom. I want to make love to you there tonight. But first, let's dry your hair. I don't want you to get a chill."

The breath caught in her throat. "Lyon, I can—"

"I know you can. I want to do it." His decision was firm, irrevocable.

He guided her to the vanity chair. He was remarkably skilled with the blow dryer and seemed to enjoy playing with her hair as he worked. Switching off the dryer, he brushed the page boy into soft feathery bangs, ends that curled gently under. "I love you," he said softly. "Don't let others ruin the last night we have together here."

Taking her by the hand he led her into the bedroom. Unlacing the tucked-in ends of the towel, he released the cloth. It fell to her ankles. The bedroom was lit only by the soft glow of firelight, and there was champagne chilling in a silver bucket next to the bed. Roses, beautiful and delicate in the lovely shades of red, pink and white, were strewed next to the soft thick quilts he had spread out on the floor. Turning her toward him, he said, "I need to know whatever hardships we might encounter, you'll stay with me. That there'll be no deserting our love if the going gets rough." His hands skimmed over her breasts, paused at the dip of her waist.

"I won't leave you," she promised. "I love you too much."

He reached for the buttons on his shirt.

"No," she said softly, firmly, "let me."

Naked, he bent to thread one of the lovely blossoms through the just-washed freshness of her hair, then with another traced her womanly form. The touch of the blossoms against her skin made her tremble. Following his lead, she picked up a rose to touch him.

Moisture bathing her thighs, she would have given herself willingly then, but Lyon was intent on drawing out their pleasure. His kisses were fierce, compelling, as his tongue delved deeper and deeper into her mouth. His hands ravaged her hair, roamed restlessly over her back. And then he was pushing her down onto the makeshift bed, gently capturing her hands on either side of her head. He stared down at her in the firelit darkness, his expression intent, searching. "I want you," he whispered. "I want you so much."

"I want you, too."

"Then make me believe it," he breathed.

His lips trailed down the side of her neck, lingered on the rapidly beating pulse, slid lower across her collarbone, to the deep V between her breasts, his tongue making hot wet forays over her skin. She arched toward him impatiently, needing the exact contact of his groin pulsing against hers. But satiation was denied her as he circled the full velvet circles of her breasts, bypassing the flowering tautness of her nipples. "Lyon, please..." she groaned.

"Say you need me." His lips claimed her shoulder, trailed lingeringly over her throat to the pulse hammering madly there, then touched the delicate rim of her ear. His teeth caught the shell-like edge, his tongue darting inside, and she shivered, her nails wantonly raking his upper arms, then his back.

"I need you."

His mouth captured hers fiercely and then with the passion he had denied her only seconds before he kissed her until she was breathless. She heard a faint groan sound deep and low in his throat as he crushed her to him, melded her softness to his strength, asking, demanding, then coaxing her to yield to love. She wanted him so badly she burned.

He broke away from her, his eyes fired with love and relief. "Colleen," he whispered. "My sweet lovely Colleen...." Hands beneath her, he slid his body down along hers, inhaling her scent. Beneath the hair-roughened surface of his skin, his flesh was warm and hard. The intimate contact, knowing where it would lead, sent fire coursing through her veins. She made a small sound of pleasure, surrendering to the sensual power he exerted over her as his tongue traced patterns across her navel, and then lower until she was writhing against him, melting like butter in the sun. Strong hands lifted her overtop of him and then they were as one.

Though he filled her completely, Colleen felt as though she would never have enough of him, stop wanting more, more.... She lowered her head, hair falling like a sheet of pale-gold satin to veil their faces.

And still he moved slowly, powerfully, claiming her inch by inch with each wave of pleasure, demanding, then coaxing until she came apart in his arms, sobbing, calling his name, giving herself to him without reservation. And only then did he give in to his own climax, the passions that held them both captive.

He held her until they both slept. Drowsy, she heard him whisper as she slipped into sleep, "Somehow, we'll find a way to make this love of ours work."

When she awoke splinters of dawn were filtering through the drapes. Colleen sighed her resignation and her sorrow as she realized at last the time she had been dreading had come. It was time to go home.

12

"I'VE BEEN THINKING a lot about us the past few days. I don't want to lose you," Lyon confided.

"I don't want to lose you, either."

Daylight filtered in through the window, and aware of the other passengers around them, they kept their voices low.

"Marry me." His hand tightened fiercely over hers.

"You're sure that's what you want?" Knowing how opposed he'd been to just the idea of getting married a week before, she couldn't help but think her feelings and circumstance—the fact he had to return immediately to Los Angeles—were working together to pressure him into a commitment.

"I love you. I want you with me," he said firmly, his hands closing over hers. The simple contact was more intimate and reassuring than anything she had ever known. "And I think I'm right in guessing you'd never feel comfortable just living with me."

"No, I wouldn't." Seeing the article about them in the scandal sheet had made her realize that.

"Then the answer is yes?" He waited intently for her response, his eyes never leaving her face.

Her newfound love for him consumed her. The depth of her fulfillment surprised her; she'd never wanted to share her life with anyone that way. "Yes."

Oblivious to the others on the plane, he pulled her to him for a slow lingering kiss.

"There's only one problem." His expression became chagrined when he withdrew moments later. "Your business is in Columbus and my permanent home is in L.A. Where are we going to live?"

"I'll move to the West Coast," she stated with finality. "It's what Amy wants anyway."

"My house in Bel Air has plenty of room. Amy could live with us there."

"I'm sure she'd like that, at least for a little while. After she finishes high school, though, she'll probably want to move out on her own, either into a college dorm or an apartment with some other girls her own age, and I think that would be a wise choice."

"It won't be too difficult for you to let her go?"

"She needs to be out on her own. As long as I'm close enough to be there if she does need a sister, parent figure or a friend, I think we'll do fine."

"I want you both to be happy."

"I know. And your concern for Amy means a lot to me."

"Then you're not still provoked with me for casting her in my new film."

"I think my irritation faded the moment I saw how happy she was to be working for you. It was probably the right move for her, in all respects."

"I think it will launch her career nicely."

"But she still needs college," Colleen cautioned.

"Yes, and I'll do my best to encourage her to continue her education."

The No Smoking and Fasten Seat Belt signs flicked on. As they adjusted their lap belts, Lyon observed compassionately, "I know moving your business won't be easy. If you like I can help you set up your own West Coast branch of Trendsetter."

"Thank you, but it won't be necessary. I'll just sell out, probably to Blake, and use the proceeds to begin again. He's been thinking of opening his own salon for some time now, but has put it off, mainly because he hasn't wanted to fool with the paperwork and the hassle of establishing a clientele. And since he runs the Trendsetter in my absence, he's a natural to take over the reins."

"You won't miss the Midwest?"

"No. And at any rate, we'll still have the Chandler-family farm to go back to whenever Amy and I do feel the need to come back to our roots."

The flight attendants moved up and down the aisle, collecting empty glasses and napkins. Lyon turned to her, anxiety reflected in his eyes. "I think it will be terrific if you open your own salon in Los Angeles, but on one condition."

Alarm bells sounded in Colleen's head. "What kind of condition?"

"I want you to be free to travel with me. Whenever I go out of town, I want you to go with me."

She swallowed hard. The wearying affects of traveling most of the day suddenly hit her full blast. "You mean commute weekends?" she said slowly.

He commented as if the answer was obvious. "No, I mean be with me full-time. As in wherever I go, you go."

"Kind of like a helpmate," she responded sarcastically.

"I wouldn't put it that way."

"I'm sure you wouldn't, as long as we give first consideration to your career and second to mine." Her voice was icy with contempt.

"Wait a minute, Colleen. I've never been a male chauvinist—"

"Then don't become one now," she shot back emotionally, unable to prevent her tone from rising. His brows shot up. Obviously she was not the only one who was close to losing her temper. *Get hold of yourself*, she thought. She was sure that once he understood how she felt they would be able to work something out. Carefully she tried to explain her position. "It's going to take me time to build a new clientele. I can't go with you on location after location and still set up and then run a conventional business in L.A. with any success."

His jaw was set stubbornly, as if he was girding himself for an argument. His level glance said he intended to win.

"Then you can work for me again."

"As much as I enjoyed being on the set of *Hearts in Jeopardy*, Lyon, it's not something I would choose to do full time. I like being my own boss. I'd feel like a fifth wheel trailing you around." If the darkening of his eyes was any indication, he thought that was a lot of nonsense. Nonetheless she asserted in her most authoritative voice, "I like working with a variety of people during the day—ordinary people. But I'm not a technician. I can and will help out creatively when needed, but as for tagging after stars day to day, combing out their hair repetitively between shots, it wouldn't be the same as what I do now. I wouldn't be challenged or satisfied creatively."

"I don't disagree that professionally I am offering you much less. But think about what we would have personally."

"Would you give up your career to come and make commercials in Columbus, Ohio?" She questioned defiantly with narrowed eyes.

Without inflection he replied, "You know what I do for a living. That can't and won't change."

Abruptly it seemed they were on the verge of losing everything they had worked so hard to nurture and discover the past weeks. A feeling of anguish she'd never before known threatened to overwhelm her. Her calm nearly shattered, she said softly, "I know that and I'm willing to work around whatever difficulties we might encounter. But I'm asking you to make some concessions, too."

"I thought I already had." His tone was curt.

"By asking me to marry you?"

He said nothing. The confirmation was in the icy unresponsiveness of his eyes. Colleen ran a shaking hand through her hair. Tears of remorse blurred her eyes. She knew what it had cost him to ask her to marry him. She loved him for that more than he knew.

"Look," he said more gently, "I know I'm asking a lot. But I want to be with you. I want this marriage to work. I've seen too many other couples break up because the people weren't together for months on end."

She recalled what he had said about his first wife refusing to travel with him. Desperately she tried to compromise, "You're right. Especially in the beginning we do need to be together. I could take some time off."

"I'm not talking about temporary or stopgap measures, Colleen. I'm talking about the rest of our life together!"

She didn't like the picture he was painting. "You're talking about some sort of outdated idea of marriage that doesn't even exist anymore. Where the man is the breadwinner and the woman takes care of the hearth and home, period!"

"You're exaggerating. I never asked you to give up your work altogether, just tailor it to fit our needs."

"While you go on just as you are." There was rancor in her tone and he said nothing. Searching for a plausible way by which to ease the differences of opinion between them, she said in a low tormented voice, "Look, maybe if I met you on weekends—"

His mouth tightened impatiently. "It wouldn't work. Oh, you'd fly to see me for the first few months, but then a crisis at work would keep you home. Or I'd have one that would keep us apart. And what about when I have to leave the country? That happens, too, you know. We film in Africa, Mexico, England.... You can't just get there in two or three hours' time. You'd hardly be with me before you had to go back."

It all seemed hopelessly complicated. Yet she held out hope. "Then we'll take that in stride, too." Her knees were shaking and it took all of her strength to keep them from knocking together. "Don't ask me to give up everything I've worked for." She couldn't and wouldn't do that for anyone. And especially not for reasons that were as selfish as his. But time was running out; they were getting closer and closer to Columbus. She could see buildings, trees and factories out the window, and the curling tail of the Sandusky River.

"I'm not asking you to quit work. Be reasonable. You can always work on my set."

"It's not enough. I have to have something of my own!" He said nothing in response. "I can't live the way you're asking me to." Her lips felt numb. The words sounded wooden.

His tone was roughly cynical, his jaw hard as granite. "Colleen, I've been through this before. You haven't. Believe me, a long-distance marriage is no marriage. I don't want the loneliness, the pain."

"What are you saying?" Her throat ached with defeat.

"Simply that I want you with me, all the time. If you can't give me that…" His voice trailed off with a finality that chilled her. There would be no marriage if she didn't comply with his demands.

"Lyon, don't do this to me. Don't make me choose." She was furious and overwhelmed by a sense of betrayal. Yet thinking back, she recalled there had been signs along the way. He had tried to tell her at odd intervals how he felt. And there was no doubt about it, his previous marriage had left him bitter and distrustful of two-career marriages. Even if she could convince him intellectually what he was asking of her was antiquated and ridiculous, she wasn't sure she would ever be able to convince him in his heart. And without his conviction that their marriage could work...

Tears blurred her eyes as the jet bumped down on the runway. She felt pushed into a corner, like a small animal frozen helplessly in the headlights of an oncoming car. The plane taxied down the runway and came to a halt.

"I'm not asking you not to use your talent, just to combine it and or align it with mine, so that maybe we could work side by side," Lyon continued more gently, squeezing her hand between his. "I'm convinced our parents were right, making the changes they did, accommodating the marriage union first rather than expecting the relationship to take all the blows and short-changes and still survive. I want a happy life for us."

"One where I make all the major sacrifices," she protested, unable to keep the sarcasm from her tone.

"If I didn't think you could be happy with me, I wouldn't be proposing. But be reasonable," he said softly. "I can't make movie after movie in Columbus, Ohio. You on the other hand can use your skills on the set. At least that way we could be together."

"I love being with you, but you're asking me to give up a career I've spent ten years building, the work that has sustained me through tragedy and disappointment and left me feeling fulfilled as a professional. Simply doing sets and comb-outs for the same small group of people doesn't compare with the kind of diverse work I do at my shop. It's like comparing the work of an ordinary ranch hand to that of a rodeo star. They both ride horses, but there the similarity ends.

"To even think about doing basically repetitive styling months on end is depressing, and it would ultimately affect the quality of our relationship. I'd resent you for what you were doing for me. I don't want to see our love destroyed by degrees. Because, like the erosion of soil or rock, that damage is irreparable. To me, it isn't worth the risk."

"You could do everyone else's hair, too," he suggested desperately.

"Oh, right. I can just see the crew lining up with you behind the scenes shouting, 'Get your hair cut, please! Colleen must have enough to do! Please, everyone, let's keep my wife busy!' It's nepotism in the worst possible form, catering that has to be done to appease the boss's wife. The crew would end up hating me and I'd feel humiliated, too!"

Sighing deeply, he glanced out the window of the jet. "Even if I wanted to make a major change now—

which I don't—I'm committed to the studio for the next four years."

There was a fact she could deal with. "You'll be out of town a lot?"

He nodded. "A minimum of six to nine months out of every year, sometimes for months on end, depending of course on the subject matter and type of film."

"Well, there goes that. I can't begin a business, given those absences, much less have a prayer of establishing a regular clientele for myself. The success of a salon depends on the customer's faith in the person who runs the business." She looked thoughtful for a moment. "I suppose I could hire someone competent to manage a West Coast establishment, but that would take away all the pleasure and satisfaction of owning a salon."

He shrugged, obviously wishing they could discuss something else. "So why bother? Why not just simply work for me and make the best of it? I know it's not an ideal situation, but it's better than nothing. It's better than us being apart."

"Is it? How happy do you think either of us could be if you were working full-time at a job you loved and I wasn't?"

Silence fell between them. His pleading glance belied the flat, uncompromising tone of his voice.

"So call me a jerk. I'm selfish and in love enough not to want to live without you by my side."

"And the bottom line is I'm expected to be amenable!" She released a shuddering breath. "I don't see how it will work if I'm not happy in my career, too, and what you've outlined thus far doesn't leave open the possibility for any other outcome. Damn it, Lyon, whether you want to admit it or not, you've reduced my life's work to an avocation, at least in your estimation."

He said nothing. Clearly, he felt she was being unreasonable. He had offered her the moon and she'd responded with. . .questions, problems, anxieties.

"Maybe we're moving into this too fast," he said irritably. He looked through his pocket for the boarding pass and ticket for his next flight. Colleen couldn't believe he was going to leave her in the middle of such a terrible crisis!

"You're going on to L.A.?" Colleen said tersely at last.

He nodded grimly. "I've got meetings at the house scheduled all day tomorrow, studio business concerning arrangements and potential problems with my next film that can't be put off." He cast a harsh look toward the terminal. In that instant she saw Columbus as he must, a small, dull midwestern town. "You're welcome to come with me, of course."

His voice unexpectedly became full of entreaty and understanding for the emotional upheaval she was going through. "Let's not leave it like this between us. Come to Los Angeles with me," he pleaded softly.

"I'd like to, but..." Exhaustion washed over her. "I don't want to argue any more, Lyon. I think if I went with you that's all we would do. I need time alone." She glanced down at her hands. Her voice was strangled with the depth of her pain. "Maybe it would be better for us if we had a few days apart."

A sound of exasperation hissed through his teeth. Now he was furious with her. "What would change in those few days?" he shot back crisply, once more the powerful man capable of masterminding multimillion-dollar film projects. "You either love me enough to make the sacrifice or you don't," he stated frankly. "I won't accept a life any other way."

Then it really was over. Part of her was too numb and too distressed to really comprehend what was happening. She knew the real pain and the tears would come later, probably as nonstop as his next flight. Tiredly, she admitted, "What you want from me, I just can't give."

His eyes darkened into the dullness of disbelief and a cold fury that could not be abated. Escorting her from the plane, he said curtly, "If you want me, you know where to find me." Judging by the betrayed look in his eyes, she was no longer sure he would be waiting for her with open arms if and when she did go to him. Colleen turned away without another word. She'd be damned if she'd give him the satisfaction of seeing her cry.

13

"IF YOU ASK ME, you and Lyon both want everything too perfect," Amy said hours later when Colleen told her via long distance how badly she and Lyon had parted. "Whatever happened to give and take? And making do with whatever time you do have together? Dad was gone a lot, too, but he and Mom were happy. We were happy."

Colleen's hand trembled where she clutched the telephone cord. "He wants me to give up my independence—at best run a business from afar."

"Marriage involves sacrifice. And I would think if you loved him you'd willingly make whatever adjustments were necessary to your career. Look how much you gave up to take care of me." Amy was silent a moment, and when she spoke again her voice was soft, cajoling. "Remember Mom talking about how hard it was when she became a political wife, how much struggle it involved, learning to entertain properly and campaign? But it was worth it to her; she grew as a person. I'm not saying you're going to have to give up as much of yourself in order to be married to Lyon, because I don't think that will happen, once you've established the fact a marriage between you, however crazy in terms of living arrangements, will work. You won't have to be an appendage to him."

"I guess it sounds selfish, but I don't want to lose myself. My whole identity is wrapped up in what I do for a living. My business anchors me personally. It gives me a sense of really helping people, making a difference in their lives by influencing how they look and feel about themselves...." It was difficult to imagine how she would manage to maintain a positive self-image without that professional satisfaction. "I don't want to become one of those Hollywood wives who spend the majority of their time shopping on Rodeo Drive."

"We all change as life goes on. But the essential kindness and generosity within you won't go away, whether you choose to work or not. You know that, too. So what is it? Is it the fact he's divorced?" Amy continued to obliterate her misgivings one by one.

Colleen was silent a moment as tears misted her vision. "He threw away one wife when the marriage didn't work."

Amy's exasperated silence told Colleen she was off the mark there, too. "If you're looking for absolute guarantees, you won't find that, either. The best you can do in any endeavor is take one day at a time. Being married probably isn't easy. But does anything worth having come without effort? I'm sure everything will fall into place, if only you love him enough to take the risk. That's the bottom line, Colleen. Do you love him?"

The answer was yes. With all her heart and soul.

Amy took her sister's silence for confirmation and made a sound of extreme vexation. "Then for pity's sake, Colleen, go to him and tell him so. If I had what you and Lyon have been given," she said firmly, "I certainly wouldn't throw it all away over a minor disagreement on how the future should be arranged."

"I guess we are being mule-headed."

"That's the understatement of the year!"

"Tell me something. How'd you get so smart?" Colleen asked wryly, glad she had followed her instincts and talked to her sister the moment she got home.

"Remember all those movies I've been watching? The good ones always have a lesson about life—so do the modern films worth seeing—that's how you tell a good script from a mediocre one. Besides, I've been thinking a lot about you and Lyon. I'm convinced you belong together. And for your information, so does everyone else on the *Hearts in Jeopardy* set. Word there is he's never been so happy."

As always her sister had cheered her. "Amy, thanks for listening, for understanding. . ." For holding her hand during the jitters. She was suddenly glad they were both going to be living in Los Angeles. As sisters, they could help each other out a lot, and the sibling support system they had worked out was invaluable.

"Just get on a plane and get out here," Amy urged. "This is no time to converse with your fiancé on the phone. I'm sure Lyon wants to see you, too."

Colleen couldn't have agreed more. "I'll fly out first thing tomorrow morning," she promised. Perhaps by then Lyon would have had a chance to cool off, too. Maybe they could work out a way to be together. Maybe, just maybe, there was a way she could establish another business that would still give her a sense of creative accomplishment, yet allow her to be free to travel with Lyon wherever he went. It was worth puzzling over....

Less than twenty-four hours later, Sam McCreary met her at Lyon's Bel Air home. "Well, aren't you a sight for sore eyes." Taking her by the hand, Samantha led Colleen into the living room where they settled at different points in the sectional sofa. "I presume you're here to see Lyon," Sam said softly. "You just missed him."

Colleen bit her lip in exasperation. "The studio said he was working at home today."

"He was. In fact we just finished. He had a dinner engagement this evening with Roxanne Stuart."

"The film star?" Vaguely she recalled the photo of her in *Celebrity*. Had Lyon sought solace in an old friend, or had he sought more than platonic consolation?

Sam nodded. Reading Colleen's anxiety, she continued frankly, "Roxie and Lyon dated a while back when she was doing another picture for him. It didn't last long. But they've remained good friends. The studio would like her to do another comedy with Lyon directing. She's nervous about getting typecast as the dumb blonde—she did that number on television for five years running, you may remember. But she's perfect for the part. For the studio's sake, Lyon's gone off to do a little hand-holding and convincing."

Sam spoke so matter-of-factly, Colleen knew in her gut there was nothing to be jealous of. Still…they had parted so badly, neither having much hope the situation between the two of them could be resolved.

"There is nothing between Roxanne and Lyon," Sam stressed, reading Colleen's anxiety. "To be honest, they'll be lucky if they can get through the evening. Lyon's been a bear ever since he came back."

"That bad, hmm?"

"That bad." Sam paused. "Look, I have the name of the restaurant where he's dining, if you want to go. I know he wouldn't mind. Lyon would probably be glad to have you either join them or cut the evening short."

"No, I—" Suddenly she wasn't sure she should have been there uninvited. Maybe she should have called first. But she'd been afraid he wouldn't want to see her, that he would still be angry.

Patting Colleen's hand, Sam soothed maternally, "Maybe you're right. It'll be an early evening, if I know Lyon's current mood. He'll do business and then get out of there. Why don't you just stay here?" the older woman urged confidently. "That way you'll be able to talk privately when Lyon does show up."

"You're sure it's a good idea? Maybe I should just go back to my hotel." Suddenly she was a bundle of nerves.

"If it'll make you feel better I could call the restaurant and tell him you'll be here waiting."

"No, I—I don't want to interfere with his business meeting. I'll just wait," Colleen decided at last.

"You're sure?"

She nodded. "I'll be fine." Reassured, Sam left.

By twelve-thirty that night, Colleen was beginning to regret her decision not to inform Lyon of her presence. Her reasoning had been she wanted to see the look on his face when he arrived, before he had a chance to assume a defensive pose. If he still loved her, surely that would show. If not, if he'd truly given up on them in his heart, well, she guessed she would know that, too.

She'd already been through two carafes of coffee, read every magazine in sight and had her fill of television. Even the butler, who had stayed on in case he could be of service, was beginning to openly feel sorry for her. Finally, at one-thirty, Colleen called Lyon's service, hoping to pick up on where he was, and was told he was "unavailable for the rest of the night, was accepting no calls and could be reached on the set through his office after nine o'clock the next morning." A sick feeling settling in the pit of her stomach, Colleen thanked the operator and hung up.

So he'd used that same excuse when he had wanted to be alone with her for a romantic evening. So he'd dated Roxanne Stuart once. It didn't mean he was sleeping with her again. And even if he was, he had no commitment to Colleen. Not after the way they had parted.

And even if he had slept or was sleeping with Roxanne, it probably didn't mean anything. None of the other women had. Then again, if he'd gotten over Colleen that quickly, maybe their love hadn't meant much to him after all.

This wasn't helping; she decided to stop thinking about it.

It was a valiant try, but it failed miserably.

Four in the morning came and went.

The butler gave up and went to bed. Colleen dozed fitfully on the couch. By dawn she had decided enough was enough. Lyon wasn't coming home and chances were he had no interest in coming back into her life, either. For that, she had no one to blame but herself. He had been straight with her from the very beginning about what he needed in a woman. She just hadn't been able to give him the requisite devotion. Meanwhile, the self-flagellation had to end. She'd humiliated herself enough for one day. She called the airport, arranged to take the first flight out and then called the salon to tell them they could begin scheduling appointments for her again early the next day. Regardless of how Lyon felt about her, she still had her business. She wouldn't let that go down the drain, too.

"YOU KNOW you could look a little happier to be here this morning," Blake chided as Colleen stalked silently into the salon.

"Sorry." She forced a smile that fooled no one. "I see the Trendsetter is still standing." Regardless of her absence. She walked to her station and began organizing her equipment. Maybe Lyon had been right. Maybe she could have started a business and run it from afar. It would have been better than living the rest of her life alone.

"We're fine," Pansy commented, slipping into a chair and crossing her legs, ankle over knee. "The question is, how are you?"

Nosy as Pansy was, it was comforting to know some things hadn't changed. It was good to be with friends. Blake gave her a searching look.

"I'm fine," Colleen lied. But her words rang flat.

"You don't look fine," Blake observed critically.

"Jet lag," she pronounced.

"I take it that means your trip to L.A. didn't go well?"

"Let's put it this way. There's no sense flogging a dead horse."

"The going was that rough?"

The disappointment had nearly killed her. But she didn't want to discuss it. Sauntering over to the appointment book, Colleen stared down at the open pages. Where her roster of clients should have been written was an erasure-smeared mess, with the initials H.D. scribbled over it. Aside from the fact they never referred to clients by initials only was the question of time. The client had reserved the entire 9:00 A.M. to 6:00 P.M. slot.

"Who's this H.D.?" she asked.

Blake shrugged. Pansy got busy sorting her clips, gels and hair dyes.

"Okay, so much for the twenty-thousand-dollar question. What did the client want done?"

Blake frowned, said dryly, "They said something about 'the works.'"

Well, whoever they were, whatever they were, they were due now. Colleen glanced at her watch, then up at the door. Her breath caught in her throat, held.

"Sorry if I'm late. I got held up at the airport," a masculine voice drawled from the portal. The shop door shut none too softly. Everyone turned at once to see a man with wheat-gold hair and captivating amber eyes lounging insouciantly in the doorway. Colleen's throat was dry, rendering her temporarily speechless, but eventually she composed herself and spoke. "Let me guess. You're H.D."

The teeth flashed white. "Hollywood Director in the flesh."

She thought of how he'd treated her the last time they'd been together, the ultimatums he had thrown down, the whole night spent waiting for him in his home. She thought of the *Celebrities* photo of him and Roxanne Stuart. The message he had left with his answering service.

She tossed down her comb, her temper and the jet lag taking hold, saying to no one in particular. "Forget it. I'm not touching his hair or anything else on his person." If he wanted a cut, wash and dry, he could go somewhere else.

"Now, boss," Blake soothed warningly.

Lyon merely grinned and crossed one ankle across the opposite leg. Blake, Pansy and Lyon exchanged now-what-are-we-going-to-do-with-her glances. Her temper rose further when she realized both her top stylists had been in on the gag all along. The

clients were stupefied, the receptionist and shampoo girl equally spellbound by Lyon's magnetic
presence.

Unfortunately for her, never had Lyon looked so
handsome. His clothes were straight out of *Gentleman's Quarterly*. Dark pants, ecru silk shirt, coor-
dinating narrow tie all complemented perfectly a
mocha-and-cream tweed blazer that hugged the
width of his shoulders, then flared out to perfectly
frame his lean hips and narrow waist. He looked as
if he hadn't slept much in the days they'd been apart,
though. Lines of fatigue curled around his mouth
and eyes.

Lyon shrugged, slipping out of his coat, and loos-
ening his tie a notch. "Any takers?"

Blake said, "Sorry, I'm all booked up."

Pansy grinned with sudden inspiration. Colleen
glared at them both. "What did you want done?"
Pansy turned to Lyon flirtatiously. And though
Colleen knew Lyon wasn't the punk-loving teen's
type—indeed Pansy already had a steady beau—her
blood simmered hotly.

Lyon turned back to Pansy, eyeing her now in-
digo-blue-and-lavender-streaked black hair. "I don't
know." He seemed foolishly willing to leave his looks
up to her discretion. "I've been thinking my hair's a
tad, too...midwestern. Know what I mean?"

Colleen knew Lyon was teasing. Still...

"I sure do," Pansy replied, looking him up and down. The young stylist turned to Blake. "What do you think? Maybe some henna? A little bright orange? You know, Lyon, we have some of the same Egyptian dye here that Lucille Ball uses on her hair."

As he shrugged and started forward, Colleen had the uneasy feeling that Lyon might really let them do it.

"Sure, why not. I've always wanted to take a walk on the wild side."

So he wanted to part with that glorious shimmering shade of wheat gold. So what? What was it to her? She didn't move a muscle.

Lyon shot her a glance, the challenging glimmer in his gold-flecked eyes goading her.

"It's your life, your hair," she said nonchalantly.

Something hardened in him then. Striding toward Pansy, he said, "I'm all yours. I don't think I need a shampoo though...just the dye...."

The seconds drew out as Pansy painstakingly mixed up the paste. Ready, she covered Lyon's shoulders with a protective cape.

"Wait!" In a panic, Colleen surprised herself by stepping between Pansy and Lyon. Not that beautiful hair. They couldn't ruin that beautiful hair.

"I knew you loved me," Lyon said softly, casting her an admiring glance. Her heart slammed against her ribs. Her love for him was warm and palpable inside her.

Everyone clapped and laughed. Colleen blushed fire-engine red as Lyon stood and ripped off the cape. Pansy peered into the mirror, then stared thoughtfully at the bowl of henna in her hand. "I wonder, maybe a little carrot orange, mixed in with the purple, black and blue...." She went off to the back to begin experimenting.

Needing reassurance that Lyon was really there with her and not merely a figment of her imagination, Colleen touched him. Because of the crowd of spectators, she contented herself with a light skim from forearm to wrist, finally clasping and entwining his fingers with hers. Her heart hammering wildly in her ears, she couldn't tear her eyes from his profile, nor deny the joy that flooded her at just the sight of him. He smiled down at her, looking as relieved and happy as she felt, and then his arms came around her, cloaking her in warmth and love. For long moments they clung together, not speaking, not talking, not kissing, just being there, together once again.

When Colleen finally looked around her, Pansy appeared to be about to faint. Blake just smiled and draped a smock over his gaping client's shoulders. Clearing his throat, he gave a conspiratorial wink, then suggested mildly, "Hey, boss, why don't you show Lyon the new software we've got for the computer."

She nodded, wiping at the tears of happiness flooding her eyes.

"Good idea." Lyon decided for both of them, grasping her elbow. He took two swift steps forward, towing her along. "I know you came to see me in L.A."

"Then you know why I left, too." Had he come to spell it out for her? To flaunt his new love in her face?

"I can imagine what you thought, but I wasn't with Roxanne Stuart all that time."

Heart pounding, she waited to hear his explanation.

"I took her home at ten-thirty. The reason I was unavailable that night was because I was baby-sitting Peter Dalton. Marcy finally went into labor and, as happened the last time, Nick completely lost his cool. He called me in a panic, this time not because Marcy refused to go to the hospital, but because Peter's regular sitter was still sick and their neighbors were out of town. I agreed to stay with him until Marcy's mother could fly in from Seattle to take over on the home front." He grinned.

"You're kidding."

"I most certainly am not. And if you don't believe me, you can check the hospital birth records. At 5:45 A.M. the Daltons welcomed a new baby girl into this world."

"How is Marcy?"

"Anxious to get home to her typewriter, as usual. She's already talking about an idea for her next screenplay."

"And the baby?"

"Healthy as can be and cute as a button. They named her Emily Lynn. The Lynn part after me. Marcy said that was as close as any girl of hers was going to get to having a 'Lyon' in her name. Anything else you want to know?"

"Uh...no."

"Good, because there's a hell of a lot I want to say to you. And it's all about us—meaning strictly private."

Flushing, Colleen led Lyon into the supply room. He shut the door behind him, leaned against it and with one swift motion brought her into his arms. "Before you say anything, I want to apologize. I was a total jerk the other day."

Tears of happiness misted her vision. "So was I."

His eyes probed hers, searching for an answer, for confirmation of their love. "I never should have asked you to give up everything to be with me."

"I never should have refused. But if you felt that way, why didn't you call me sooner?"

He shrugged and gazed down at her with remorse. "Because I kept remembering one of our first conversations, when you told me how you had dreamed of having kids, a husband, the home with the white picket fence. I knew that, however much I tried, right now I couldn't give you that kind of life.

"It wasn't until Marcy went into labor and I was called over to help out that I began to realize just what I was giving up. Later, the next morning, when I was able to take Peter over to the hospital to see his new baby sister, I talked to both Nick and Marcy about how they made their two-career marriage work. I realized belatedly that compromise was something I had not given a lot of thought to. That just because my first marriage failed, it didn't mean ours would. I realized how much I wanted to have what the Daltons had for us.

"I came home, found out from Styles you'd been there—who felt I had treated you abominably, by the way—and I immediately called and booked you for today and put myself on the first flight out. I love you, Colleen, and if you'll have me, I still want to marry you."

His arms tightened protectively around her. She leaned into his strength, relishing the security, the sense of belonging. Her cheek rubbed the smooth wool of his blazer.

"You have a right to have your own life aside from me," he continued. "Your independence and spunk are the qualities I love most about you."

She tilted her head back so she could better study his expression and said seriously, "That doesn't change the fact that you're a famous director. Being involved with you is going to mean certain adjustments on my part. I'm going to have to change my life-style. I'm going to have to put the marriage, not my career, first. It doesn't mean I'll neglect my life's work, just that I'll keep it all in perspective. Marriage means sacrifices, Lyon, on both our parts. And being married to someone famous means being in the limelight some of the time. I'm willing to adjust to publicity and interview giving."

His hands laced through her hair on either side of her head. His mouth worshiped hers briefly, tenderly, atoning for past hurts.

After what seemed like a very long time, he promised, "I'm willing to do whatever it takes to make you happy. And if it means underwriting a Trendsetter salon in Los Angeles and your staying there most of the time, then so be it. We'll find a way to make it work, Colleen. We'll both commute."

But she didn't want his to be the only concessions. She admitted softly, "Frankly, the business of running a shop day to day was getting a little tedious. That's one of the reasons I took so many out-of-salon appointments before. I liked the change of pace, meeting new people. But equally important to me is designing hairstyles that fit a person's life-style, personality, facial features, bone structure and individual hair type.

"I'd like to sell out the shop here to Blake and get into a new business—a beauty-consulting operation that would travel from city to city. I could work in conjunction with major hotel chains, salons and department stores, give workshops for professionals, not just in the hair-care field but in the areas of makeup and wardrobe selection, too. I could plan my schedule to mesh with yours and work wherever you're filming without feeling like a fifth wheel. And we could still be together every evening, just as if we both worked nine to five in the same city. And if you need me I could work on your sets, too, as a consultant."

"Or with other directors," he said. "I showed a couple of my friends the rushes from the town-council scene in *Hearts in Jeopardy*. They wanted to know who did the punk looks. Your services are already in demand."

The touch of his hand on the soft skin of her throat was almost unbearable in its tenderness. His lips brushed hers as he spoke. "May I take this to mean you've changed your mind and will marry me?"

She rose on tiptoe and kissed him until both their mouths were burning, their bodies melded together as one. "If you'll have me."

"I couldn't live without you." He moved his mouth over hers, devouring her lips with a hungry kiss that told of the depth of his need. His arms tightened around her.

"I don't ever want to be without you, either," she confessed, her voice ragged. "So, no more long-distance romance?"

"No more long-distance romance," Lyon echoed firmly. He delivered a series of slow, shivery kisses that left her clinging to him, supremely happy. "However we live our lives, we'll live them together. And I'll be there for you, too, Colleen," he promised. "On this day and forever."

Harlequin Temptation

COMING NEXT MONTH

#85 LIFETIME AFFAIR Patt Parrish

Ben and Caroline were neighbors battling a storm together to save his beach house from destruction. And when the waves subsided, it was clear that the attraction between them was as inevitable as the tides. . . .

#86 WITHOUT A HITCH
Marion Smith Collins

She was footloose and freewheeling down the interstate to a new life in Florida. But one glance in her rearview mirror and Libby found herself rerouted. Suddenly, falling in love was an unavoidable detour!

#87 FIRST THINGS FIRST
Barbara Delinsky

Chelsea's job was to track down missing children—not runaway executives. But the moment she found the renegade, hidden away in a remote Mexican village, she knew what she'd been searching for . . . all her life.

#88 WINNING HEARTS Gloria Douglas

Six years ago Elizabeth's childish advances had been spurned by rugged John Logan. Now a glamorous model, she was ready to take on the arrogant cattleman. The result was an electrifying showdown!

TEMP-85-88

WORLDWIDE LIBRARY IS YOUR TICKET TO ROMANCE, ADVENTURE AND EXCITEMENT

Experience it all in these big, bold Bestsellers— Yours exclusively from WORLDWIDE LIBRARY WHILE QUANTITIES LAST

To receive these Bestsellers, complete the order form, detach and send together with your check or money order (include 75¢ postage and handling), payable to WORLDWIDE LIBRARY, to:

In the U.S.
WORLDWIDE LIBRARY
Box 52040
Phoenix, AZ
85072-2040

In Canada
WORLDWIDE LIBRARY
P.O. Box 2800, 5170 Yonge Street
Postal Station A, Willowdale, Ontario
M2N 6J3

- -

Quant.	Title	Price
_____	**WILD CONCERTO**, Anne Mather	$2.95
_____	**A VIOLATION**, Charlotte Lamb	$3.50
_____	**SECRETS**, Sheila Holland	$3.50
_____	**SWEET MEMORIES**, LaVyrle Spencer	$3.50
_____	**FLORA**, Anne Weale	$3.50
_____	**SUMMER'S AWAKENING**, Anne Weale	$3.50
_____	**FINGER PRINTS**, Barbara Delinsky	$3.50
_____	**DREAMWEAVER**, Felicia Gallant/Rebecca Flanders	$3.50
_____	**EYE OF THE STORM**, Maura Seger	$3.50
_____	**HIDDEN IN THE FLAME**, Anne Mather	$3.50
_____	**ECHO OF THUNDER**, Maura Seger	$3.95
_____	**DREAM OF DARKNESS**, Jocelyn Haley	$3.95

	YOUR ORDER TOTAL	$_____
	New York and Arizona residents add appropriate sales tax	$_____
	Postage and Handling	$___.75
	I enclose	$_____

NAME _____

ADDRESS _____ APT.# _____

CITY _____

STATE/PROV. _____ ZIP/POSTAL CODE _____

WW3

Take 4 books & a surprise gift FREE

SPECIAL LIMITED-TIME OFFER

Mail to   **Harlequin Reader Service**®

In the U.S.	In Canada
2504 West Southern Ave.	P.O. Box 2800, Station "A"
Tempe, AZ 85282	5170 Yonge Street
	Willowdale, Ontario M2N 6J3

YES! Please send me 4 free Harlequin Temptation® novels and my free surprise gift. Then send me 4 brand-new novels every month as they come off the presses. Bill me at the low price of $1.99 each—a 13% saving off the retail price. There are no shipping, handling or other hidden costs. There is no minimum number of books I must purchase. I can always return a shipment and cancel at any time. Even if I never buy another book from Harlequin, the 4 free novels and the surprise gift are mine to keep forever.

Name   (PLEASE PRINT)

Address   Apt. No.

City   State/Prov.   Zip/Postal Code

This offer is limited to one order per household and not valid to present subscribers. Price is subject to change.   DOHT–SUB–1

M

Harlequin Intrigue

Because romance can be quite an adventure.

Available wherever paperbacks are sold or through

Harlequin Reader Service

In the U.S.
Box 52040
Phoenix, AZ
85072-2040

In Canada
5170 Yonge Street,
P.O. Box 2800, Postal Station A
Willowdale, Ontario M2N 6J3

INT-6